NONVIOLENT RESISTANCE TO THE NAZIS

NONVIOLENT RESISTANCE TO THE NAZIS

GEORGE PAXTON

YOUCAXTON PUBLICATIONS

OXFORD & SHREWSBURY

Copyright © George Paxton 2016

The Author asserts the moral right to
be identified as the author of this work.

ISBN 978-1-911175-18-6
Printed and bound in Great Britain.
Published by YouCaxton Publications 2016

The author thanks Navajivan Trust for permission to quote extracts of Gandhi's
writings as they appear in *Non-violence in Peace and War, Volume I. 1962*

Contents

To Ruth and Clifford

Preface

This is not a book of original research in the sense of presenting information hitherto unpublished, rather it draws upon a wide range of published material to present a perspective on the Nazi era which is rarely put forward. One aspect of the subject is the hiding and rescuing of persecuted Jews, and opponents of the regime. There is now a vast literature on this aspect of nonviolent action and only a representative selection of these actions is described here. The other major aspect of nonviolent action is resistance by the general population on their own behalf. This appears to be less well documented, unless it was simply less common than rescuing of others. Perhaps future research will give us a different perspective but the examples we have at present are sufficient at least to demonstrate the potential of this relatively novel way of struggle.

Underlying this approach is the belief that the traditional method of dealing with large scale conflict has such massive defects, both practical and moral, that it makes sense to explore alternatives with urgency. This book does not deal with the prevention of conflicts which is obviously an extremely important aspect of the subject, possibly more important than the one presented here. However, if it can be demonstrated that nonviolent methods of resistance are available to civilian populations and may overall be more successful than violent resistance this should open the way to a more civilised approach to conflict in human society.

Introduction

While examples of nonviolent action can be found as far back as the ancient civilisations it was only in the 20th century that systematic studies of it developed. While the usefulness of nonviolent action (NVA) in resolving certain conflicts – both in democracies and authoritarian states – is gradually being recognised, it is not generally considered a realistic substitute for armed force if the conflict is extreme. The case most commonly cited as showing its limitations is that of Nazi Germany. President Obama in his Nobel Peace Prize acceptance speech in 2009 while praising nonviolent action added: "A nonviolent movement could not have halted Hitler's armies". Perhaps most people would take that simply as a statement of fact. Citing the Nazis is still taken as showing the ineffectiveness of nonviolent action when up against a ruthless opponent, and so its very limited usefulness.

Yet a considerable amount of NVA was used against the Germans in occupied countries of Europe during the Second World War and in Germany itself by the regime's opponents. The extent of it and the degree of effectiveness varied from country to country but in some form or other it was present.

Nonviolent action was undertaken by single individuals as well as groups ranging in size up to large segments of the population. The participants were in some cases deeply religious (Catholic, Protestant, Orthodox Christian, Muslim or Jewish), others were atheistic communists, others were humanistic liberals or democratic socialists. Some were pacifists, more were not. Cardinals and professors and diplomats took action, sportspeople and actors also, as did housewives and mothers, as well as children. The extent of resistance varied considerably from country to country, depending on the characteristics of the population but also on the structure of the occupying regime which was not uniform and varied considerably from country to country.

It is clear that the NVA that was used against Nazi German forces, even in the country where it was most widely used – probably Norway – was insufficient to expel the occupier. But if it had been used even more widely and systematically as a nonviolent strategy the outcome could have been more satisfactory. Certainly a determined and courageous populace can produce tremendous difficulties for an occupying force who must have a substantial level of cooperation from the occupied population to function. Nor is extreme repression by the occupier the answer to their problem as this is likely to provoke stronger opposition from the occupied population. A difficulty for the occupying forces is how to respond to NVA, something which they are not trained to deal with.

The greater part of this study describes actual cases of nonviolent resistance during the Nazi era, or as Jacques Semelin prefers to call it in his *Unarmed Against Hitler* – 'civilian resistance'. I prefer to use the expression 'nonviolent resistance' in order to link it with potential action which is used as a superior ethical method and not just expedient action. Throughout most of this study 'nonviolent resistance' is used loosely to mean resistance that does not involve physical violence.

Included is the resistance to the Shoah, the attempt to destroy the European Jews which took place during the War. A very substantial literature on the efforts to rescue Jews trapped in Nazi Europe now exists as survivors have made public their stories towards the end of their lives. The efforts of Jews to save their own lives and that of other Jews is also part of the story.

The latter part of the study puts all this in the context of nonviolent theory particularly that of the slightly different approaches of American academic and campaigner Gene Sharp and of Mohandas Gandhi who was both theoretician and activist.

The earlier part of this study shows that it is certainly possible to use nonviolence in a very oppressive situation – it is a realistic option, although the outcome will not always be what is hoped for; but then neither does the use of violence always lead to a satisfactory outcome. From a recent study of NVA in the 20th century it appears that NVA in diverse situations is more likely to lead to a successful outcome than the use of violence. The book concludes with a consideration of how different a Gandhian approach to resistance to the Nazis would have been compared with a purely pragmatic approach.

Resistance in Pre-War Germany

Resistance to Nazism within Germany itself preceded Hitler becoming Chancellor in January 1933 but resistance became increasingly difficult as the state became Nazified. The Reichstag fire on 27 February 1933, whatever the cause (a Dutch communist was accused), was exploited by the regime and used as a reason for rounding up enemies of the state such as some 10,000 communists and the banning of the Communist Party (KPD). In the last multi-party election to be held, on 5 March 1933, the Communist Party attracted 12% of the votes and had achieved 81 seats which were however cancelled. The German Socialist Party (SPD) was even larger with about 1 million members and achieved 18% of the vote and 120 seats. The National Socialist German Workers' Party (NSDAP, the Nazi Party) had 44% and 288 seats, the largest number of seats but not an overall majority. But Hitler managed to get an Enabling Act passed with the support of the non-socialist parties making him effectively dictator. Socialist opposition was not as strong as it could have been because of antagonism between the KPD and the SPD. Trade unions were also opponents of the Nazi Party so on 2 May trade union offices were occupied by Stormtroopers (SA). The SPD was treated less harshly than the KPD by the new regime but it agreed to be dissolved on 22 June 1933. Although the number of German workers was large and the membership of socialist parties was fairly large those prepared to take any kind of action against the regime was very much smaller. Nevertheless some statistics show a fair level of active opposition: by 1935, 5708 distribution centres of illegal documents were known to the Gestapo; in 1936, 1.6 million leaflets of the communist and socialist parties were confiscated. The communists formed cells in the factories and former SPD members kept in touch through sport and social clubs. 62 socialist MPs of the last Reichstag before Hitler were to lose their lives.

The traditional German elites in the army, civil service and business largely supported Hitler after he came to power but by the late 1930s many began to have doubts as he appeared to be leading the country to war. However with the military successes in the early stages of the war Hitler retained his general popularity. When reversals on the war front appeared groups of conspirators became more active.

The Protestant churches, with a membership that was nearly twice that of the Catholic Church, were divided with, on the one hand, the development of the pro-Nazi 'German Christians', and on the other, those clergy (6,000) who tried to protect their independence by forming the Emergency Association for Pastors. The pastors of the latter organisation drew up the Barmen Declaration in May 1934 asserting their prime loyalty to Christ and the Church. Their numbers grew to 17,000 clergy at its peak. When the German Christians' deputy leader August Jäger tried to impose an oath of loyalty to Hitler on the clergy there was widespread opposition and when the bishops of Württemberg and Bavaria publicly protested they were placed under house arrest. Opposition continued to such an extent that the bishops were invited by Hitler to an interview which was followed by the dismissal of Jäger from his post. The acceptance by Hitler of the existence of a pro-Nazi German church was an interim measure as he intended to eliminate Christianity from Germany in the longer run. In 1936 non-Aryan Christians (former Jews) were excluded from the clergy and offices in the Protestant churches; consequently an organisation was set up to help such people emigrate and to raise funds for them. After August 1939 schools were established to cater for Christians of Jewish descent. American and British Quakers aided emigration and later provided hideouts and also food and clothing.

One pastor who resisted was Martin Niemöller, a First World War veteran, who was imprisoned in 1937 and was not released till the end of the war. However, like so many Christians his first concern was the independence of the Church and it was only during his imprisonment that he realised his former viewpoint was too limited. After the war he became an active peace campaigner. The theologian Dietrich Bonhoeffer was staunchly anti-Nazi and initially a pacifist who moved eventually to the position that Hitler should be killed. The failure of the conspiracy of 20 July 1944 led to his arrest, with many others, and his eventual execution.

In 1936 the Government attempted to replace Catholic symbols with Nazi ones in Catholic schools. This was met with priests in the area of Oldenburg in North Germany protesting at the interference; children went to school with crucifixes; church bells were rung in protest, and even some women Nazi Party members did not obey the directive and some Nazi Youth members similarly. As a result on 25 November the Nazi leader in Oldenburg called a public meeting in a large auditorium and announced that the policy was changed. Similar reactions occurred in some other towns. In March 1937 Pope Pius XI issued an encyclical *With Burning Concern* accusing the Government of violating the Concordat between Hitler and the Catholic Church (20 July 1933) which delineated separate spheres of influence – religious and political. Although many individual priests, monks and nuns also actively protected Jews, the Church as an institution was weak in its defence. Higher priority was given to defending their own faith and organisations.

Baptists, Methodists, Mormons, Adventists all discriminated against Jews in Germany with only the Quakers and Jehovah's Witnesses being consistent in their support. Jehovah's Witnesses were the staunchest opponents of the regime. There were around 20,000 in the country and they were imprisoned in labour camps from 1935. They refused any compromise and by 1945 were spread around all the concentration camps in occupied Europe. Witness children were often taken from their parents to be brought up in homes where the parents were Nazi Party members.

An early individual opponent of the Nazis was the lawyer Hans Litten (b.1903). On graduating he established in 1928 a law firm along with Dr Ludwig Barbasch which defended opponents of the Nazis who had been charged with offences. In 1931 Litten subpoenaed Hitler himself to appear as a witness in a case against two SA men. He intended to show through his questioning that Hitler was encouraging violence against his opponents and this, he hoped, would turn more moderate Germans against Nazism. He succeeded in embarrassing Hitler but his hoped for result did not follow. Hitler did not forget him and on the night of the Reichstag fire Litten was arrested and thereafter kept in various concentration camps. After repeated brutal treatment he ended up in Dachau concentration camp where, having given up hope of survival, he hanged himself in February 1937.

In 1936 in Marburg, Judge Wundheiler refused to sign an oath of loyalty to the regime and was dismissed from his post. He managed to get a job as a court messenger which was the most favourable outcome to be expected.Wundheiler and Litten were very much exceptions among German lawyers.

Among the young the regime admitted that only about 10% of students were Nazis in 1935. One secret youth movement called Edelweiss was widespread; another called Packs had about 2000 boys and girls in 1939; in 1938 there was a treason trial of 50 of them in Leipzig and 52 in the Rhineland. A Catholic youth group, the Gray Order, in which Willi Graf of the later White Rose group, was a member, suffered many arrests in 1937-8.

One example of cultural resistance was the artistes at the Katakombe cabaret in Berlin led by Werner Fink, a comic actor and satirical cabaret performer. They continued to openly criticise the Nazis until 1935 when they were closed down. Fink survived the war and lived till 1978.

A half-Jewish woman, Edith Wolff, resorted to 'pin pricks' against the regime. She started sticking pieces of paper with messages in catalogues and indexes in public libraries where Nazi books were referred to. She got stickers from a pharmacy with the slogan 'Danger – Poison' and attached them appropriately. Another method she used was sending short typed witty messages of protest to Government departments and the media. She continued similar actions for years.

Resistance also came from a section of the political and military elite of Germany who were repelled by the extreme actions of the regime. One form of effort taken was the approach of Wehrmacht officers, including General Franz Halder, to Pope Pius XII early in the war to mediate with the Allies as the conspirators were willing to attempt a coup to displace Hitler and the Nazis. The British Cabinet considered this on 17 January 1940 but decided to take it no further.

Between 1933 and 1939 about 225,000 people were sentenced for political crimes. Gestapo records of 10 April 1939 showed 162,734 people in Protective Custody. In May 1939 alone, 1,639 people were executed for political offences.

General Nonviolent Resistance

The Second World War began on 1 September 1939 with the shelling of the Polish port of Danzig by a German warship. It had been preceded by the Soviet-German Non-aggression Pact a week earlier. By 27 September the unequal conflict was over as Poland surrendered. At this point disagreements within the German high command led to postponements of the intended attacks on France and Britain. Some months later, fearing a British occupation of Scandinavia, Hitler decided to occupy Denmark and Norway which were attacked on 9 April 1940; Denmark surrendered almost immediately but Norway fought on till 7 June.

On 10 May at last came the attack in the west. The Germans had 141 divisions while the Allies (France, Britain, Belgium, Netherlands) had 144. The Germans were superior in aircraft numbers (about 4,000 to 3,000) and the Allies were superior in tanks (3,300 to 2,300). In spite of the roughly even balance of numbers the German army swept through the Netherlands, Belgium and Luxemburg and into France by 17 May thus by-passing the massive French fortifications of the Maginot Line on the German-French border. France surrendered on 22 June, and also concluded an armistice with Germany's ally Italy, which had invaded the south of France, on 24 June. The air battle intended to destroy the British air force prior to invasion of Britain, which lasted from July to October 1940, failed and Hitler turned his attention elsewhere. In April 1941 Germany went to the aid of Italy in its attempt to take Greece and in brief campaigns took in Yugoslavia also. On 22 June 1941 Germany broke the Non-aggression Pact and attacked the Soviet Union making rapid advances taking in Lithuania, Latvia and Estonia. Germany was now master of continental Europe.

At its greatest extent the population of the German occupied territories was 260 million which was twice the population of the USA at the time.

In **France,** the north and west of the country, about 60% by area, came under direct German control while a French Government was established in July 1940 at the spa town of Vichy in the centre of France as a collaborationist regime with First World War hero Marshall Pétain as the head. Political parties were abolished in the Vichy area, and the authoritarian regime dismissed more than 2,000 civil servants, and 3,000 French Jews were removed from public office. The Vice-Premier, Pierre Laval believed in German supremacy and was an enthusiastic collaborator. The French people were stunned by the rapidity of the defeat but the armistice may well have been a relief to most French people who remembered the horrors of the Great War. Thus it was a while before resistance developed, indeed the existence of the French Vichy regime gave some legitimacy to the occupation.

The first demonstrations against the occupation did not take place until 11 November 1940 when several hundred students and children marched down the Champs-Elysées singing the Marseillaise and waving flags. Ninety schoolchildren and fourteen students were arrested.

In exile General de Gaulle, who was not well known initially, was frequently to call for demonstrations: for example on 1 January 1941 he appealed for people to stay indoors, and on 1 May 1942 there were many silent marches in the Vichy zone with thousands participating. There were tens of thousands of participants in Lyon and Marseille and thousands in other cities who booed the name of Laval and cheered the name of de Gaulle. De Gaulle came to represent uncompromising Free French resistance to German occupation. Each 14 July, the national holiday, people displayed their national colours and marched past national monuments. Families often dressed their first child in blue, their second in white, and their third in red.

On 10 May 1941 a strike by French miners against food shortages began and by 4 June about 100,000 miners (80% of the total) were on strike. Communists were prominent in instigating the strike. This prompted hundreds of arrests, including women, who had urged firmness in the strike, and 235 people were deported, of whom 130 never returned. The strike was over by 10 June but it did result in more food coupons being provided.

Following the occupation many refugees fled to Bordeaux where the Portuguese Consul General, Aristides de Souza Mendes, issued thousands of documents to Jews, socialists and other enemies of the Nazi regime between February and June 1940. These visas and false passports enabled them to get to Spain and Portugal. This was against orders and the Consul was removed from his post. (See Case Studies) The First Secretary of the Spanish Embassy in Paris, Eduardo Propper de Callejo (d.1972) similarly signed passports, using both hands, amounting to 1500 during 4 days.

The Catholic Church as an institution saw Vichy as a bulwark against Communism which was in the eyes of many Catholics a greater threat than Nazism. Cardinal Baudrilliart gave his blessing to the Legion of French Volunteers against Bolshevism in July 1941 as it set out for the eastern front. But individual Christians including Catholics played a major role in rescuing. Two major organisations providing escape routes for those in danger were the Inter-Movement Committee for Evacuees (CIMADE), created at the start of the war for Alsace and Lorraine refugees and which later helped many others. Similarly the Christian Witness, which was run by Father Chaillet of Lyon with the support of Cardinal Gerlier, was very active in rescue work. During the war these organisations helped about 12,000 people to flee to Spain and 10,000 to Switzerland.

After being out of office for a period, Pierre Laval was reinstated by the Germans in April 1942 and he tried a voluntary recruitment of labour for the Germans which resulted in a total of only 17,000.

This was therefore replaced by compulsory recruitment which was to apply to men aged 28 to 50 and unmarried women aged 21 to 35 and by the end of 1942 the number demanded by the Germans of 250,000 was reached. Workers' departures sometimes led to large scale demonstrations. Further German demands for labour led the Vichy Government to conscript young people born in 1920-22 for labour in Germany lasting two years. A common reaction was to avoid conscription by escaping into the mountains and forests with the support of the rural population. Some of them formed guerrilla resistance groups called Le Maquis. Further resistance support came from civil servants providing false papers and employers ignoring requests for personnel. Some police also gave prior warnings to those about to be detained. One attempt to deport French citizens led to an invasion of the Montluçon train station on 21 October 1943 with most deportees escaping as a result. Although the majority were later captured it nevertheless gave a boost to morale.

An individual case of resistance was by the psychiatrist Adelaide Hautval (1906-88) who was born in Alsace and spoke German as well as French. Her father was a Protestant pastor. She was arrested in Paris while visiting her ill mother without having permission, and after protesting at the treatment of Jewish prisoners she ended up in death camps including Auschwitz. Here she used her medical knowledge to help ill prisoners but refused to participate in the medical experiments conducted there. A Nazi doctor said to her: "You cannot see that these people are different from you?" She responded: "There are lots of other people different from me, starting with you". She managed to survive until the liberation. [Fogelman p.196]

More than a thousand underground newspapers were produced in France during the occupation although many were short lived. *Défense de la France* went through 47 editions of 300,000 copies in 1943-44 and was produced in its first year by students at the Sorbonne. The press was kept in a cellar of a laboratory with access being by a key held by a student called Hélène. When the production was moved to a Resistance printshop circulation reached 450,000. Acquiring paper for such numbers was a major undertaking as well as the distribution. One of the distribution offices mailed between 10,000 and 40,000 to influential figures and was headed by Geneviève de Gaulle, the General's niece.

As Jacques Semelin points out, overall the Vichy collaboration was greatly to the benefit of the Germans: the supply of industrial and agricultural goods, of labour, help in rounding up Jews and dissidents, and also to a significant extent it gave legitimacy to the occupation and thus discouraged resistance. [Semelin p.18]

Throughout the occupation, **Belgium** was directly administered by the Germans. The Government took the decision to go into exile while King Leopold decided to surrender his forces and stay in Belgium. The cabinet and some parliamentarians and civil servants fled to France, moving several times ahead of the German forces and ending up in London as the Government-in-Exile. However most Belgian civil servants and judges remained in post in the hope that they could mitigate the impact of the occupier by pointing out the unconstitutionality of undesirable legislation. The Germans removed any legislative power and increased the executive power of the General Secretaries who were heads of the civil service departments. The judges, headed by the First President of the Supreme Court of Appeal, remained in post but ultimately were unable to block the Germans' aims. For example, the General Secretaries tried to prevent the anti-Jewish orders of October 1940 claiming that this would break equal treatment legislation. Nevertheless the General Secretaries were pressured into applying the orders even although they were not actually published. In May 1942 all criticism of the regime by the Supreme Court judges was made a punishable offence. In response the judges stayed away from work. This was followed by their arrest and the threat of the death penalty. However the threat was not carried out, they were released and the Court went back to work. Because the Belgian judges did not want a complete break with the occupiers they had to give way on other matters such as the deportation of Jews and workers for Germany.

Belgian railways' director-general refused to release railwaymen for employment in Germany, and the mayor of Brussels, J F van de Meulebroeck, refused to dismiss senior staff and so was removed from office; when he asserted that he was the legitimate mayor he was arrested and his city administration was fined.

The public made their views clear about the new regime when on 11 November 1940, the anniversary of the end of the First World War, there were major demonstrations in the main cities. Miners and metal workers, who produced what was essential to the Germans, became discontented over their pay and the inefficient distribution of food and in January 1941 about 10,000 miners came out on strike over a tax imposed by the General Secretaries; then workers at a large munitions factory struck over food rations. On 10 May tens of thousands of miners came out. This led to concessions similar to those in France at the same time. Belgian coal production in the winter 1941-2 dropped by 36% mainly due to deliberate slow working.

Underground newspapers were widespread during the occupation and were distributed in a variety of ways. Some were passed from hand to hand to friends and acquaintances, some were actually posted to prominent figures, and many were distributed on the street while lookouts were posted. One particular issue of *Le Soir* which was controlled by the occupiers was sold at newspaper kiosks but when read it was revealed as a forgery giving news of the resistance.

In December 1941 lecturers at Brussels University stopped teaching in protest at Nazi staff being admitted; teaching continued clandestinely with 65 teachers who enabled 400 students to complete their studies by giving 110 courses to groups of six. In spring 1943, 6,000 students went underground to avoid labour service.

Belgium was a strongly Catholic country. Half of the population had a Roman Catholic education and Catholic unions were the largest. Some Roman Catholics collaborated but rectories and convents often hid Jews and resisters. Initially Cardinal Joseph van Roey was cautious but he wrote confidential letters of protest to the head of government, General Falkenhausen. Van Roey gradually changed to more open opposition and 15 March 1943 was a turning point when the Cardinal made a strong public declaration against forced labour. This had a substantial impact on the Belgian population and resulted in increased resistance to forced labour and resistance in other sectors.

In April 1943 workers struck against labour conscription. 60,000 workers stopped work in the industrial area of Liège, which then spread to Charleroi, La Louvière and other centres. The Germans decided to suspend their intended action.

After the invasion of the Grand Duchy of **Luxemburg** the royal family and government went into exile in Britain. The aim of the Germans was to incorporate Luxemburg along with Alsace and Lorraine, into the Reich itself. The country had mines and metallurgical industries so was of industrial value to the Germans. The occupiers were interested in Luxemburg for another reason, namely, the perceived racial similarity of the people to the Germans, so Gauleiter Gustav Simon organised a census to be in effect a referendum on the incorporation of the country into the Reich. But the census laid down that Luxemburgisch could not be entered as one's language. In spite of that rule when the questionnaires were analysed it was found that 96% of the urban population and 99% of the rural population entered Luxemburgisch as their native language. The response of the occupiers was to arrest several thousand people and imprison or deport them.

Being in need of new troops for the eastern front the regime decided to give the citizens of Luxemburg German nationality and then recruit the young men into the Wehrmacht. Strikes against conscription began on 30 August 1942 in the Esch mining area and then spread to Luxemburg city. Students were particularly active. There were hundreds of arrests, 40 people were deported and 21 young people were executed. Thousands more went underground.

The **Netherlands** was invaded on 10 May 1940 and the Government surrendered only four days later. Queen Wilhelmina and the Government went into exile in London. Rotterdam was heavily bombed. Most of the merchant fleet escaped to Allied ports.

There was much collaboration in Holland during the occupation but also substantial resistance. General public opinion swung between accommodation and opposition until 1943 when it began to veer towards the latter. During the early part of the occupation many Dutch factories produced for the German war-machine and food and raw materials were exported to Germany. This was a major demand of the occupiers in the occupied countries.

On the first morning of the invasion a chain letter appeared with readers being encouraged to copy it and pass it on. This first was followed by others. The originator was Bernhard Ijzerdraat who called the campaign Gueux ('Beggars') after a 16th century resistance group against Spanish occupation. He was arrested in November 1940 and executed along with fourteen others.

A few weeks later the Germans banned the flying of flags on the birthday of Prince Bernhard, 29 June, who was in exile in London, but many people carried or wore a carnation of red, white or pink on the day. General Henri Winkelman, ex-commander-in-chief of the Dutch Army, went to the palace and added his name to a declaration of independence. This led to the mayor of the Hague being removed from office and Winkelman being sent to Germany where he spent the war in detention in various places. He had earlier urged Dutch people not to produce or supply goods that would help the German war effort.

The civil service General Secretaries mostly collaborated with Reich Commissioner Arthur Seyss-Inquart, an Austrian. He appointed four Commissioners to supervise different sectors of the civil service. The police service was re-organised with pro-Nazis. Seyss-Inquart gave members of the civil service the opportunity to resign without punishment but expected those who stayed on to be loyal to the new regime. Most stayed in post. C Ringeling, Undersecretary for Defence, was dismissed after protesting about munitions factories being taken over. In June 1940 the Dutch Parliament was suspended and the General Secretaries were given increased powers under the direction of the Commissioners. Thus it was the Dutch who supervised the first decrees discriminating against Jews and also enforcing compulsory labour in Germany. The contradictory position of the General Secretaries led most of them eventually to resign by the end of 1943.

When the Jewish President of the Supreme Court, L E Visser, was dismissed in November 1940 his colleagues did not protest. Because of the weakness of the Supreme Court its members were eventually dismissed by the Government-in-Exile although not till 1944. Opposition did not form into an efficient network and the Dutch Nazi Party, led by Dr Anton Mussert, had 110,000 members at its peak. Trade union party members quietly resigned from their organisations. Chair of the Social Democratic Party, Koss Vorrinck, refused collaboration. The Communists had hidden or destroyed their records and the Socialists dissolved their party in mid-1940. The Roman Catholic and Protestant trade unions acted similarly.

The churches declared Nazism to be incompatible with Christianity and the RC bishops sent a pastoral letter forbidding the priests to give the sacraments to National Socialists. The churches forbade their members to assist in the detention and deportation of Jews, or to help those searching for those evading work conscription or any other collaboration. In February 1943 they encouraged their members to commit civil disobedience even at the risk of losing their jobs or incurring other penalties only stopping short of risk of death or deportation to a concentration camp. Hundreds of ministers were arrested and 43 Protestant and 49 Catholic priests lost their lives resisting the Nazi state.

In 1941 the Undersecretary for Education and Science, van Dam, dismissed staff of Leyden University who were anti-Nazi and tried to replace them with pro-Nazi members but this was thwarted by the threatened resignation of the entire University staff. In May 1942 a professor of constitutional law was dismissed and this time 80% of the staff resigned bringing the University to a standstill. Students refused to take an oath of loyalty to the regime so 85% of them were ordered to report for labour service. This prompted 6,000 students to go underground and staff volunteered to teach and hold examinations in secret. After the war the exam results were declared valid.

There were protests against the takeover of the press and radio and clandestine newspapers reached a total of 1200 to compensate. Most editors of the labour press resigned – one committed suicide. Artists and actors refused to join the Nazi Chamber of Culture.

In March 1943 all students had to sign an oath or be conscripted for labour service. Only 15% signed. At the Catholic University of Nijmegen it was 2%.

The largest strike in occupied Europe began on 30 April 1943 with half a million participants which started in response to the call for military service of the former Dutch soldiers who had been taken prisoner in 1940 but then released. Strikes took place in the mining area of Limbourg and the Philips factories of Eindhoven. People came out onto the streets in the cities. Unusually some peasants and delivery people refused to bring milk to the cooperatives. Street protests were attacked and more than 100 people were executed but only 11,000 servicemen checked in for deportation. The strike was over by 8 May. Although the strikes lasted only a few days much of the Dutch population were henceforth more willing to help those trying to escape forced labour.

An individual example of symbolic resistance was displayed by Diet Eman, a bank employee in The Hague who knitted and wore a jumper to work which was orange – the royal colour, with flowers of red, white and blue – the national colours. Eman became heavily involved in hiding and rescuing people sought by the occupiers.

Hiding people sought by the occupiers was developed on a large scale and for this money was needed. In June 1941 the Roman Catholic Church established a relief fund which collected 15 million guilden in three-and-a-half years. A Protestant relief fund was established too and it distributed hundreds of thousands of guilden. A National Relief Fund was also set up to provide for families of seamen who were abroad, workers on strike, and those in hiding. It became recognised by the Government-in-Exile and money was raised by loans from well-to-do Dutch people and was underwritten by the Government-in-Exile. By the end of the war about 84 million guilden had been raised. About 15,000 men, women and children cycled the country distributing to those in need. An important role was played by the medical profession but initially the Dutch Society for the Promotion of Medicine or NMBG took a compromising line. Then a new organisation, the Medical Front (MF), was created by a few pro-Nazi doctors in November 1940. The NMBG in May 1941 accepted one of the MF members to participate in plans for its future direction but the Germans then announced that the role of the MF member would be to direct the changes in the NMBG and that meant excluding Jewish doctors. Opposition to this grew during the summer and a mass resignation movement began. By the end of the summer most of the 5,700 members had resigned from the NMBG. The Catholic medical association followed suit. On 14 September 1941 a clandestine medical body formed, called Medisch Contact (MC) with rules that no Jewish patients were to be reported to the authorities and the identity of wounded patients was not to be revealed. On 16 December a letter signed by 4,261 doctors was delivered to the Reich Commissar affirming freedom from political interference. The official Chamber of Dutch Physicians which the Germans had formed was boycotted but the Germans started fining those who had not joined and for each refusal to join another fine was added to the previous one. The resisting doctors now decided to resign from medical practice. On 24 March 1943 more than 6,000 doctors, that is almost all practising doctors, took this action, although they continued to look after their patients. In summer 1943, 360 doctors were arrested and their surgeries were closed. But they were gradually released and although the official organisation continued to exist it was agreed that the doctors need not join it to practice. The outcome for the Dutch medical profession was very similar to that of the Norwegian teachers described elsewhere.

In September 1944 a rail strike was started which lasted till the end of the war but the Germans retaliated by banning all goods traffic and this resulted in a famine which severely affected the Dutch population in the remaining months of the war.

The **Channel Islands** were very isolated after occupation and there was a very high ratio of Germans to the native population so collective resistance was ruled out by the local administration.

The occupation was a relatively mild one but due to being cut off from normal supplies of all kinds daily living became increasingly difficult.

Slave labourers brought in to build fortifications were treated harshly and although they were kept apart from the islanders escapees were sometimes successfully hidden by the locals.

(See The Model Occupation.)

In **Poland** Nazi oppression was severe in the extreme with the Germans determined to destroy Polish culture and people as they considered the Poles to be a racially inferior people and intended the land to be settled by ethnic Germans. One of the earliest attacks was on 5 November 1939 when all members of staff at Cracow University were summoned to a lecture theatre to be addressed by an SS officer. He accused them of not seeking permission to inaugurate the academic year and of being hostile to German scholarship. As he spoke the campus was occupied by SS troops and they proceeded to arrest 171 members of staff to be deported to Sachsenhausen concentration camp in Germany. Its precious library was also sent off to Germany and the University was closed down. In the same month secondary schools and higher educational institutions were closed and the teaching of Polish language and history were officially abolished. Scientific institutions were closed down. However technical schools remained open and so they were used clandestinely by the Poles to continue teaching Polish culture. Legal, medical and religious institutions were attacked and individuals were arrested and some executed. Radio and theatre were also closed down.

But this repression led not to destruction of Polish culture as intended but rather to more unity among the Poles and the setting up of alternative institutions. In Warsaw from 1940, theology, law, medicine, arts and other subjects were taught in the underground. By 1944 more than 200 lecturers were teaching and 4,235 students enrolled for 1943-44. In makeshift schools 19,000 teachers taught about one million pupils. Tens of thousands of illegally printed textbooks were distributed and parents were asked to continue paying fees while the teachers were paid salaries. In Warsaw alone 8,000 school leavers sat examinations. By 1942 Cracow University had been revived underground and degrees were awarded and research papers published. A total of 282 scientific handbooks and monographs were published. Before entering a university course students had to sign a declaration which read:

"My sole purpose in applying for the courses is to acquire an academic education. I swear, first, to preserve the strictest secrecy about the times, venues, attenders, titles, and contents of lectures and courses, not only in the company of strangers and persons unknown (not to mention enemies of Poland), but also in that of uninitiated friends, and to beware of referring to the same in conversation, especially in public. I swear, secondly, to obey the rules and regulations laid down by the academic authorities in regard to life and work at the university. I swear, thirdly, that I will show myself a true Pole and join no organisation hostile to our country, whether public or secret; and that, so far from working for the cause of the alien occupying power, I shall be mindful only of the welfare of the Polish nation and state. So help me God." [Werner Rings p.182]

In fact a clandestine state developed in cooperation with the Government-in-Exile led by General Wladyslaw Sikorski which had been formed shortly after the occupation and embodied the four largest political parties. There was even a functioning parliament in Poland, as well as a civil service, a secret army, a civilian resistance directorate, and a coordinating committee for other groups such as economic, educational, religious and other spheres. Scientists continued to carry out research, and judges tried criminals, enemy spies and war criminals. Substantial funds for this underground state came from the Government-in-Exile. The extreme repression of the occupiers had led to the solidification of the resistance.

The Sudetanland, the ethnic German part of **Czechoslovakia,** was ceded to Germany by the Munich Agreement of 29 September 1938 and six months later the whole of the country was occupied. A spontaneous display of patriotism took place that year on the anniversary of the founding of the independent state, 28 October, when several thousand citizens demonstrated dressed in national costume. National Solidarity badges were worn upside down, SN standing for Smrt Nemcim or Death to the Germans. Police tried to disperse the crowd and a worker and a medical student, Jan Opletal, were killed. Opletal's funeral on 15 November was attended by 3,000 students. This was orderly to begin with until storm troopers began to provoke the students and then the police attacked. Students overturned the car of Police Commissioner Karl Frank.

Hitler used this as justification for repression and the universities were closed permanently, nine student leaders were executed and 1,200 sent to concentration camps.

On the first anniversary of the occupation (March 1940) the streets of Prague were empty while people stayed at home. Unlike most public gatherings pilgrimages were permitted so on five occasions as many as 100,000 gathered and sang national songs. In summer 1940 Prime Minister General Elias joined the gathering. On Hitler's birthday the population largely stayed away from the military parades and instead lay wreaths on monuments to Tomas Masaryk, first President of Czechoslovakia. On the anniversary of the Munich Agreement the streetcars in Prague were empty in response to a request from the underground.

General opposition continued with a boycott of German films and art exhibitions and when German soldiers appeared on film they were jeered. Athletic contests between Germans and Czechs were abandoned due to unruly behaviour by the audiences. An attempt to measure facial features of school children for racial classification was abandoned due to the non-cooperation of doctors.

Denmark was occupied with little resistance on 9 April 1940, indeed the citizens of Copenhagen awoke to find German soldiers on the streets. The Danish Government had decided that the country was so weak militarily that it was pointless to resist. However this attitude was not appreciated abroad and the Danes were criticised for not resisting. The occupation was unique in that Denmark retained a largely independent government – headed by the Socialist, Thorvald Staunting – until 1943. A memorandum of 9 April 1940 recognised Danish authority in internal affairs which included the police force. The Germans looked on the Danes as fellow Aryans but there were other reasons for the leniency that was convenient to the occupiers. But nearly two-thirds of the Danish fleet headed for Allied ports.

Nevertheless there was some resistance, for example, handwritten leaflets appeared in Copenhagen on the first day of occupation headed "Ten Commandments for Passive Resistance" which were produced by a group of 17-year-old students. The Commandments were:

1. You must not go to work in Germany or Norway.
2. You must do bad work for the Germans.
3. You must practice working in slow motion for the Germans.
4. You must destroy all the tools and machines that could be useful to the Germans.
5. You must try to destroy anything that can be profitable to the Germans.
6. You must delay all transports to Germany.
7. You must boycott German and Italian newspapers and films.
8. You must buy nothing from from German shops.
9. You must behave with the traitors according to what they deserve.
10. You must protect whoever is pursued by the Germans.

(Semelin, pp.36-37)

These Commandments may not have been very widely observed but it indicates that some of the populace were thinking in terms of resistance of a nonviolent nature.

There was a striking case of symbolic resistance in September 1940 when Danes gathered together to sing; in Copenhagen Park 150,000 came, there were 20,000 in Ebsjerg, and it spread to almost every town and village; around the country possibly as many as two million Danes participated, which would be two-thirds of the population over age fourteen. Other actions were having gardens with flowers in the national colours, and conspicuously not going into cinemas until the German newsreels had finished.

A difficulty arose for the Government in January 1941 when the German Minister in Copenhagen requested that the Danish Navy place eight torpedo boats at the disposal of the German Navy, adding that this would not infringe the neutrality of Denmark. The Danes replied that this would break agreements made at the start of the occupation. The Germans replied that they were not required for military purposes as they were to be used for training but they were again refused. The German Minister then called on the King and mentioned that someone in Berlin might decide that coal deliveries to Denmark might be stopped. In the meantime the Danes had dismantled the guns and torpedo tubes on the ships and removed them, along with navigational equipment. At that point the Government decided to compromise and the boats were turned over to German control after a demonstration on the dockside in the presence of the King who said that one day the boats would be returned to Danish control.

At the same time the Germans were pressing for a more pro-German position by the Danish Cabinet including dismissal of the Minister of Justice and the Chairman of the Social Democratic Party who were members of the Cabinet. The Government did not give way on this. John Christmas Moeller, leader of the Conservative Party and an anti-Nazi, repeatedly criticised German policy at public meetings and the Germans demanded that the Danish Government remove him from all posts he held but this was rejected by them. Moeller then heard that he was going to be arrested and sent to Germany so made plans to escape to London which he managed to do.

Another conflict arose when the Germans called on the Danish Government to introduce the death penalty for Danes who endangered the security of the occupiers, for example, members of the Resistance movement. The Germans indicated that they would have such individuals tried by court-martial if the Danes did not concede. The Danes pointed out that the public reaction to the death penalty by Danish courts would be strong and suggested the penalty in such cases be limited to life imprisonment. The Germans accepted this.

By the end of 1941 popular discontent with some of the Government's actions emerged, for example the banning of the Communist Party and imprisonment of Danish Communists, and the raising of a Danish Free Corps to fight on the eastern front, following from the German invasion of Russia in June 1941. The Cabinet had held out for some time but when the right-wing Danish Foreign Minister, Erik Scavenius, signed the Anticomintern Pact in Berlin on 25 November 1941 there was rioting in Copenhagen.

Significant concessions by the Danish Government were made on the economic front. They encouraged the migration of Danish workers to Germany (more than 100,000 went), and industrial production for Germany was greatly increased, as were agricultural exports to Germany. The occupiers also increased occupation charges.

Concerts of German music were boycotted by the public and singing of traditional Danish songs was organised instead. The civil service worked deliberately slowly. Some Danish police supplied information to resisters. Red, white and blue circles on caps began to be worn mainly by students and it was some time before the Germans realised they represented the RAF roundel. Also Danes began to give German soldiers the 'cold shoulder', for example if a German entered a shop or a restaurant the Danes would leave; or if a German spoke to a Dane he would be met by silence.

Listening to BBC broadcasts was not made illegal as it was in other occupied countries and the broadcasts gave encouragement to the population. The V-sign became widespread as it was chalked or painted on many walls and other locations. As late as March 1943 a general election was allowed to be held from which the Social Democrats emerged as the largest party with 44.6% of the vote and 66 seats while the National Socialists received only 2% and 3 seats.

When a young man was shot and hurriedly buried by the Germans there was a huge demonstration (10,000) with wreaths and a memorial service which the Germans allowed. But this led to some shooting by the troops. After a worker was shot, the next day 17,000 gathered in a quarry where Danish Nazis attacked them and this led on to other protests ending with the declaration of martial law throughout the country.

Relations deteriorated further in 1943 when sabotage became widespread. In August 1943 a wave of strikes and demonstrations swept through the country (in 15 towns). Danish shipyard workers also refused to repair German ships. In Odense, 10,000 workers gathered in the sports stadium and demanded that the German forces be confined to barracks and Danish hostages be released. The Germans gave way. On 29 August the Government ceased to function and the Wehrmacht took over while Danish armed forces were disbanded and individuals were interned. However the Danish police continued to function. The following month a Freedom Council was formed to direct the resistance, both sabotage and nonviolent.

In May 1944 Danish police refused to protect factories from saboteurs. In June sabotage led to the execution of some Danish prisoners. Also a Danish corps that had been formed to fight for the Germans in Russia returned to Copenhagen and this Schalburg corps (named after its commanding officer) instigated terror against the population. Their actions included the blowing up of large buildings in the town. This prompted a general strike during which Danish police refused to act against demonstrators. The Germans then cut off water, gas and electricity to the city. Negotiations began with the help of Georg Duckwitz, the German shipping attaché, and the public services were restored and German patrols stopped in return for the general strike being called off. In September all police were ordered to be arrested and sent to Buchenwald but only 2,000 police were actually detained as 7,000 managed to go underground.

There was an extensive underground press to support the resistance in Denmark – 538 newspapers during the occupation with a combined circulation in 1944 of over 10 million.

Norway's nonviolent resistance was one of the strongest of the occupied countries. 96% of the population belonged to the Lutheran Church and so in this as in other respects was an unusually homogenous population. It had a strong democratic tradition and a high level of civic involvement. Norway was attacked on 9 April 1940 although its army did not give up till 10 June. Although the Norwegians were Aryan, in the eyes of the Nazis, they were not treated with the leniency that the Danes were.

The invasion did not go well for the Germans. The Norwegian defence sank the German flagship with the loss of 1,600 men including most of the Gestapo and administrative officers who were to take control of Oslo. The fleet turned back and troops were flown in instead. When the Germans attacked, the leader of the Fascist Nasjonal Samling (NS, National Unity), Vidkun Quisling, announced a government and named ministers, but found that many refused to serve or could not be found. Goebbels was not pleased by this unexpected attempted seizure of power and the German Ambassador Brauer presented Quisling with a formal protest. King Haakon refused to recognise Quisling's government and he and the legitimate Government left Oslo. On 16 April Quisling was removed from his position. An Administrative Council was then set up under Supreme Court President Paal Berg. On 24 April 1940 Ambassador Brauer was replaced by Josef Terboven as Commissar of the Reich. The reaction of the civil service was mixed with some civil servants resigning, some collaborating, and some trying to defend Norway's interests while remaining in post. On 10 June the King and Government as well as the treasury left Norway by ship for Britain. Under German pressure some MPs who had remained called for the King's resignation but this was declared illegitimate by those in exile. On 25 September all political parties except the NS were banned, but the NS itself was under suspicion as developing an anti-German but pro-Norwegian nationalist stance, and so a State Council of pro-Nazis was established by Terboven.

The Supreme Court resigned on 12 December 1940 as it refused to meet demands of the occupier and Paal Berg and other judges and lawyers joined the resistance.

The Norwegian merchant navy, then the fourth largest in the world, was mostly at sea when the country was occupied. It comprised about a thousand ships and 30,000 seamen whose leaders formed an organisation called Notraship in London to administer the fleet. The Norwegian tanker fleet came under Notraship also and it carried 40% of the British Empire's petroleum until the USA entered the war.

Spontaneously, Norwegians started wearing paperclips in their lapels signifying "keep together"; in classrooms students took to wearing necklaces and bracelets made of paperclips. When they were banned, tiny potatoes on sticks appeared and the potatoes were gradually increased in size to signify growing resistance. Other symbols of opposition began to appear such as pictures of the King, royal insignia, the V-sign, flags on coat lapels, red clothing such as caps. Later, on the King's seventieth birthday, people wore flowers and hundreds were arrested, some even spending the rest of the war in prison camps.

In May 1941, 43 organisations, with a total membership of 750,000, such as civil servants, dentists, lawyers, nurses, clergy, and others, sent a statement to Terboven. Eight of the leaders were arrested and all signatories were dismissed. All resigned from their organisations. The government confiscated their funds. In June 1941 an underground Committee of Civilian Co-ordination and Resistance was set up, called Sivorg; along with a military wing called Milorg.

During 1941 school children were taken to a Nazi exhibition but their response was to look at the ground rather than the exhibits or have a competition to see how fast they could run round the exhibition hall. In school, Nazi pupils were shunned by the others and sometimes they left school as a result. A strike by actors closed down theatres in Oslo, Bergen and Trondheim for many weeks.

Early in 1942 Quisling was reinstated and on 1 February 1942 the Primate of the Lutheran Church, Eivind Berggrav, addressed a letter to the Government criticising the Quisling police, the Hird, and also affirming the right of confidentiality of pastors. As no response had been given by 9 February the document was publicly read in churches. Clergy refused to preach on the radio when it was taken over by the Ministry of Propaganda. When Quisling was formally appointed Minister President at a service in Trondheim Cathedral it was boycotted by the populace. On Easter Sunday 5 April the Church broke all ties with the State and so pastors lost their salaries. Only 50 pastors out of 850 retained their posts. Several dozen pastors were arrested and the Primate was put under house arrest. The Swiss theologian Karl Barth addressed a letter of support to the Primate, and the Archbishop of Canterbury praised the response of the Church.

Quisling tried to organise occupational groups into new Nazi associations but met with stiff resistance. The leaders of the Athletes Association were dismissed and the Chairman was imprisoned but the new organisation was boycotted and no skiing or sports competitions were held throughout the occupation. A distinguished psychiatrist, Dr Johan Sharffenberg, was very outspoken in his opposition to the Nazis and fearless. He regarded Hitler as being a paranoid psychopath and for his outspokenness received short periods of imprisonment and was removed from his post at the Oslo Asylum. Nazi professors were boycotted and Professor Didrik Seip, the Rektor of Oslo University, refused to comply with a new Board of Examiners in Law. He was imprisoned and deported to Germany but survived. Doctors refused to merge their Medical Association with the Nazi Guild of Health.

The most impressive resistance came from the schools. On 5 February 1942 Quisling created a new teachers' organisation as a pilot for the corporate state he hoped to establish. A compulsory youth organisation for 10-18 age group was also established. Most teachers refused to display Quisling's portrait, and refused to replace English with the German language. Nor did they take an oath of loyalty to the new regime. Instead, arrangements were made to send letters to the Ministry of Education repudiating the new organisation to arrive on the same day – about 4,000 letters were received. University teachers followed. Teachers were threatened with dismissal. The government decided to close the schools for a month on the pretext that there was a lack of fuel. Teachers continued to teach in homes. The closures drew attention to the protest. Parents then wrote letters of protest, about 200,000. Only a few dozen teachers joined the Nazi union. The Government responded by arresting 1,000 teachers on 20 March and deported them to labour camps in the frozen north of the country. The largest group went to Kirkenes near the Finnish border where Russian prisoners lived in terrible conditions. In spite of the conditions few teachers capitulated. The Government reopened the schools on 1 May and the teachers returned but without supporting the official union. The imprisoned teachers were gradually released. The whole Government plan had been defeated.

In December 1943, students at Oslo University found their university closed down and several thousand were arrested with hundreds of them sent to Germany. Of the remainder many escaped to Sweden but others went underground. [See General Resistance in Norway]

In **Germany** the churches were a potentially strong opposition to the regime, in fact the Nazis were more worried about religious opposition than communist. However the Protestant churches were split into a number of denominations, and the Catholic Church had compromised with the regime when Pope Pius XI signed the

Concordat negotiated by Cardinal Pacelli, the future Pope Pius XII. Nevertheless some significant opposition by Catholics did develop.

In April 1941 Gauleiter Adolf Wagner of Upper Bavaria banned crucifixes from schools and ordered Nazi songs to be sung in schools instead of school prayers. As with pre-war attempts to Nazify schools this met stiff resistance and petitions, letters, and meetings of parents made their disapproval clear. Parents threatened to remove their children from school and some wrote letters to their husbands at the front telling them what was happening at home. Some pictures of Hitler were removed and so Hitler decided to overrule the Gauleiter.

The 'euthanasia' programme, ie the murder of those with mental health problems and physical disabilities, began in October 1939 and was referred to as T4 from the address Tiergarten 4 from where it was directed. Hitler had intended from the beginning to start a euthanasia programme but delayed it until the start of the war as he feared church opposition. Six killing centres were set up and cases were reviewed by three medical experts without even examining the individuals. Initially starvation was the method used, then injections or pills, then gassing. 25 psychiatrists (7 of them Professors) organised the programme. Patients were transported by a special SS team. Relatives received letters and death certificates. Although it was done as secretly as possible it met with strong opposition as knowledge of it spread among the German population. There was even opposition within the Nazi Party, for example, Goebbels feared a reaction from Catholics, and Himmler had doubts too, as did the Army commanders fearing that disabled former soldiers would be included.

Only a few doctors protested at the programme and these included Carl Bonhoeffer, a leading psychiatrist and father of Dietrich, the pastor and theologian. A few psychiatrists refused to fill out associated forms but only one psychiatrist, Professor Gottfried Ewald of Gottingen openly opposed the killings. During the summer of 1940 an increasing number of priests and nuns brought pressure to bear on the bishops. Initially the bishops refused but on 1 August 1940 the Archbishop of Freiburg, Konrad Gröber, wrote to the Minister of the Interior. The Protestant Bishop of Wurtemburg sent letters to the Minister of the Interior and of Justice about the programme. On 9 March 1941 the Bishop of Berlin, von Preysing, made his opposition public, and on 31 July the Catholic Bishop of Westphalia, Clemens August von Galen, denounced the programme in strong terms and other bishops followed his lead. Critical sermons circulated among soldiers and they even spread abroad. Bringing into the public sphere what the regime wanted to be kept secret led to widespread opposition to the programme. Relatives became suspicious at the number of deaths occurring and other observations such as the buses leaving institutions full and returning empty. In the Bavarian village of Asberg the whole population of the village, including Nazi Party members, turned out in February 1941 to protest at the deportations. Rumours spread that the killings might extend to wounded soldiers and the elderly. Anti-regime jokes were told. Action by Pastor Fritz von Bodelschwingh, Director of the Bethel Centre in Wesphalia saved 8,000 residents through personal contact with Kurt Brandt, the head of T4. Some in the Nazi Party thought von Galen should be executed but this idea was dismissed because of his popularity and the effect it might have on morale in the armed forces. Due to the negative publicity Hitler reluctantly gave orders on 24 August 1941 to stop the programme (but with the intention of resuming it later). About 70,000 mentally and physically handicapped people had been killed. About another 30,000 were allowed to die from starvation and disease.

Suicide could sometimes be looked on as a form of resistance. In Germany more than 5,000 Jews committed suicide in the Nazi period, a rate which was well above average. In the transit camp of Drancy near Paris about 100 suicides took place in two and a half months but this was disapproved of by some inmates because the numbers sought by the Nazis would be made up with others. In camps people would walk to the fences to be electrocuted or climb up them to be shot by guards.

Members of the loose grouping known to the Gestapo as Rote Kapelle, or the Red Orchestra, forged documents, produced newspapers, leaflets and also smuggled people. Although the Gestapo considered the groups to be Communist they in fact included Social Democrats and Conservatives, and religious affiliations included Lutheran, Catholic and Jewish. In February 1942 a Berlin group produced a leaflet denouncing the regime and claiming that the Germans were losing the war. Several hundred leaflets were successfully distributed through the post to bishops, professors, doctors, engineers and other professionals. Some resisters were civil servants who had access to military information and passed it to the Allies particularly the Russians so were not strictly acting nonviolently since their information would be used by the armed forces. Scores of these men and women were uncovered and arrested in August-September 1942 in Berlin followed by hundreds of others. Many of them were executed.

One resister who operated from within the German establishment was Count Helmuth von Moltke. A member of the family of two famous Field Marshals, he had formed a discussion group on his estate at Kreisau and hence the members were known as the Kreisau Circle which included his wife Freya, who like her husband was a lawyer. He was a supporter of the Weimar Republic and opposed the Nazis from the beginning. He visited Britain several times in the 1930s and had English friends. In spite of this background, on the outbreak of war he was recruited to the Abwehr, or military intelligence, to work in the international law section. Remarkably, the director Admiral Wilhelm Canaris provided cover for several anti-Nazi conspiracies. Von Moltke himself tried to countermand various illegal military orders concerning treatment of prisoners of war and of Jews and tried to get the German forces to adhere to the Geneva convention. The Kreisau Circle discussed the principles on which a post-war Germany would be built. Although he did not approve of any assassination attempt on Hitler, he was arrested following the 20 July 1944 unsuccessful plot and executed in January 1945.

Munich University was the centre of a few examples of general resistance. Professor van Rintelan, a lecturer in Ancient Greek philosophy, one day did not appear to deliver his lectures so 50 students suspecting that he had been dismissed went to see the Rector and also demonstrated at the University entrance. The protest however did not lead to his reinstatement. The anthropologist Karl Saller did not agree that there was a fixed Nordic race and claimed that modern Germans were racially mixed. For this he was dismissed on the orders of Reinhard Heydrich. Another Professor, Heinrich Wieland, a Nobel Prize winning chemist, gave sanctuary to half-Jews by appointing them as demonstrators and allowing them to complete their studies unofficially. He refused to use the greeting 'Heil Hitler'. One of his half-Jewish students, Hans Konrad Liepelt, was arrested along with six other students for collecting money for needy Jews and other offences. Wieland provided lawyers for them and appeared for Liepelt's defence but he was found guilty and executed in January 1945. Surprisingly, Wieland managed to retain his post. The best known resistance also centred on Munich University. A group made up mainly of students took the name – the White Rose. This is described under Case Studies.

Eric Boehm, who had fled Germany as a teenager and returned as a US Army interrogator at the end of the War, tried to estimate the scale of resistance within Germany and concluded: "Over a period of twelve years almost three million Germans were in and out of concentration camps and penitentiaries for political reasons – sometimes for as little as a remark critical of the government. About 800,000 of these had been arrested for overt anti-Nazi acts, only 300,000 of them were still alive at the end of the war – so that among the 'illegals' alone 500,000 gave their lives". [Nelson pp.293-4]

Rescuing and Protecting Jews

Anti-semitism was deeply rooted in Europe especially so in eastern Europe where the largest Jewish population was located. Pogroms were familiar to many in Ukraine, Poland, Hungary, Romania and Slovakia. The Jews of western Europe were largely assimilated and that was true of Germany, in contrast to the majority of Jews of the east who were more distinct from the majority population. With the defeat of Germany in the First World War followed by economic collapse Hitler was able to intensify irrational fears and hatred of Jews and blame them for the Germans' misfortunes. At first expulsion of the Jews from German territory was seriously considered by the Nazis but no suitable homeland could be found and the practical task of removal abroad would have been formidable in any case. But persecution in Germany led many Jews to emigrate especially westwards to France, Belgium and the Netherlands; some reached the UK and USA. On 23 October 1941 the Nazis decided to stop emigration with the aim of exterminating the Jews within Nazified Europe. German Jews abroad also lost their nationality so that it became easier to seize them in the occupied territories.

[In the following, figures for populations of Jews are very approximate as different sources often give quite widely differing numbers.]

There were about 350,000 Jews in **France** in 1940 but 200,000 were foreign including 50,000 German refugees. More than half of the Jews fled to the southern zone (Vichy) following the invasion. However the Vichy Government had no interest in protecting foreign Jews so a law of 4 October 1940 authorised imprisonment of foreign Jews and as a result about 25,000 refugees from Germany were interned in Gurs concentration camp. A department for Jewish Affairs was established in March 1941 to oversee the application of legislation and consider further legislation. When Pierre Laval returned as Prime Minster in March 1942 he agreed with the Germans to deport 20,000 stateless Jews from Vichy.

In the northern zone from April 1941 Jews were excluded from a wide variety of occupations and in May foreign Jews began to be placed in camps in France. This was followed by the Yellow Star being made compulsory in May 1942. This prompted non-Jewish young people in particular to express their opposition to the discrimination by themselves displaying various symbols such as the Yellow Star, wearing a sign saying 'Negro', or putting the Yellow Star on their dogs. The majority of the population, however, were indifferent to the fate of the Jews at this stage.

On 28 March 1942 the first deportation train left Drancy transit camp near Paris supposedly for resettlement but actually for Auschwitz extermination camp. Himmler transferred command of the German police from the military to the SS. On 16-17 July 1942 a large round-up of foreign Jews began in Paris but many Jews were warned of the impending event. However one of the most notorious events of the occupation of France then occurred. Under German orders French police rounded up some 13,000 foreign and stateless Jews in Paris and took them to an enclosed sports arena, the Vélodrome d'Hiver. Thousands of people were held in extremely crowded hot conditions and kept there for 8 days. Such were the intolerable conditions that there were suicides, yet 9,000 French police did nothing to help. Only at this point did some Christian leaders protest publicly. Many Parisians hid Jews and out of 22,000 planned arrests only 12,884 were seized in the first two days. From a total of 76,000 deported during the occupation 40,000 were in five months of 1942. When French men began to be conscripted for labour in 1943 French police became less cooperative so that the Germans had to rely on the French fascist paramilitary Milice to carry out orders.

A rescue organisation, Amité Chretienne or Christian Friendship, was formed in 1941 led by Jesuit priest Pierre Chailet and Abbé Glasberg. Father Chaillet, who published a clandestine paper, helped many Jewish children in the region of Lyon. Official Church opposition was weak at first but the round-ups of July 1942 brought a change. On 23 August 1942 the Archbishop of Toulouse, Jules-Gérard Saliège, who had expressed opposition to Nazism from 1937, issued a public letter against deportations and four other bishops in the southern zone followed his example. In the north Cardinal Suhard, Archbishop of Paris wrote letters to Marshall Pétain and Prime Minister Laval (but post-war his opposition was not considered sufficient for him to be invited to the Service of Liberation in Notre Dame Cathedral).

There were only about 600,000 Protestants in France but in March 1941 Pastor Marc Boegner, President of the Protestant Federation, protested at Vichy's anti-Jewish legislation and sent two letters – one to Foreign Affairs minister, Admiral François Darlan, and the other to the Chief Rabbi Isaie Schwartz – which were made public. However Boegner made it clear that he was only concerned with French Jews not foreign, a common position at this stage. German requests for French Jews were refused by the Vichy government. On 26 August 1942, 6,000 foreign Jews were arrested in the southern zone but this was fewer than expected as many were hidden in convents, schools, monasteries and homes. On 25 September Himmler decided it was better to keep good relations with Vichy and exclude Jews of French nationality from deportation. By this time the Vichy Government knew that 'resettlement' meant extermination and therefore began to obstruct the Germans.

When the Allied troops landed in north Africa the Germans decided it was safest to occupy all of France which happened in November 1942 and this led to about 35,000 Jews fleeing to the Italian zone where they remained in safety. Under pressure from the Germans the Italians registered the Jews there and moved 22,000 of them but only to the interior of the zone. Eichmann then sent one of his aids, Alois Brunner, to Nice to sort matters out but by the time he arrived the list of Jews had been destroyed. After the surrender of Italy in September 1943 the German army moved into the zone but by then the Jews had fled to Italy itself or were making their way to Switzerland or Spain.

Two foreign relief workers who helped to save children especially were Alice Resch (Norwegian) and Helga Holbeck (Dutch). They worked mainly with Quaker organisations in southern France providing accommodation and food for children who had been moved to camps. Many of the children were Jewish and some were hidden in convents and monasteries with the support of the Bishop of Toulouse. Some were smuggled to Switzerland and as a result a few hundred were saved. Father Albert Gau with the help of a sympathetic woman opened a restaurant which served as a front for Jews and other refugees. He had a network of helpers including nuns in a Carmelite convent. Overseas assistance came from the American Friends Service Committee who were feeding 30,000 children daily in Vichy France in December 1940.

Two other foreign rescuers were an American couple, Waitstill and Martha Sharp, the former being a Unitarian minister and Martha a social worker. In February 1939 they left their two children in the USA and went to Prague in response to an appeal for people to help dissidents and Jews escape. In 1940 they spent most of the year in France helping those in danger to escape from France and also provided food and other aid. Martha arranged for 13 tons of powdered milk to be delivered to refugee children in camps. They aided a German novelist, Lion Feuchtwanger, who was on the Nazis most-wanted list to get to the USA. They also arranged for 29 children to escape by ship to the USA.

The Haute-Loire region of the southern zone was an area where many children especially were taken and settled in villages. They were helped by CIMADE (Comité d'Inter-Movements Aupres des Evacués) and the Christian Witness. CIMADE started as a relief organisation in 1939 and was led by Madeleine Barot and Pastor

François Delpech. Le Chambon-sur-Lignon is the best known of the villages but others in the Haute-Loire and nearby Cévennes region sheltered Jews and others and were not betrayed even by those who supported Vichy. Marc Donadille, a pastor in St Privat de Vallongue in the Cévennes picked up Jewish children from Aix and Marseilles and hid them throughout the region. His brother was director of the railroad and was able to schedule trains to suit escape network operatives. In Nice, Monsignor René Remond used his bishopric as a centre for rescuers. 108 children were released from a detention centre near Lyons and were sheltered in religious institutions under the protection of Cardinal Gerlier. About 7,000 Jewish children were saved by Christian Witness.

An unusual form of protection was displayed by the Paris Conservatoire which formed an orchestra of students to protect Jewish students from deportation. The orchestra toured Germany with a Jewish violinist as soloist in the Mendelssohn violin concerto.

In Paris a mosque frequented by Algerian ex-patriates became a rescue centre for Algerian Jews. They were hidden in the principal mosque and supplied with false passports identifying them as Muslims. The leading figure in the mosque was Si Kaddour Ben Ghabrit who did his utmost to give as little information as possible to the Germans who were suspicious. [The film *Free Men* directed by Ismael Ferroukhi in 2011 deals with this event.]

The French Jewish Council did not function in the way intended by the Germans – it operated as a welfare agency by running orphanages, putting Jewish children in safe houses, and sometimes managed to smuggle children out of the country.

Belgium was put under direct German rule but while collaboration was common, there was also strong resistance which grew stronger with time. Jews were fairly widely dispersed in Belgium and were in significant numbers in Antwerp, Brussels, Liège and Charleroi.

A symbolic action occurred in November 1940 in Antwerp when Jews were ordered to wear the Star of David and non-Jews responded by wearing it in solidarity. There was a resistance movement, the Independence Front, which was linked to the Committee for the Defence of the Jews (CDJ) which was founded by Hertz Jospa, a Communist Jew of Romanian extraction. When the Germans set up a Jewish Council, the CDJ managed to get a member on to the Council so that it was informed of German plans. CDJ conducted a large propaganda effort to persuade Jews not to give themselves up at the Malines Centre. They established with the help of the Catholic Church safe places such as convents and schools and hid especially Jewish children. They supplied false papers and ration cards. One feature of this movement was young women called 'visitors' who travelled around supplying food and other essentials to those in hiding. Many of the rescues were carried out by networks of Jews working with non-Jews.

Police and railway workers also helped to obstruct deportations. Railway workers helped Jews escape from trains and the police did not cooperate in the round-ups. Robert Maistriau with two colleagues in a bold action stopped a train carrying 1,600 Jews, many of them children, using a red light and then opened some of the carriages which allowed 231 to escape.

In September 1942 Cardinal van Roey, head of the RC Church in Belgium, and the Queen Mother, Elisabeth, intervened on behalf of six leading Jews who had been arrested. As a result five who were Belgian were released but the sixth, who was Hungarian, was sent to Auschwitz. The Cardinal encouraged Church institutions to shelter Jews.

In spite of 94% of Jews in Belgium being recent immigrants – Polish Jews after the First World War and German after 1933, a total of around 70,000 – and foreign Jews always being more vulnerable than native Jews yet about half of all Jews in the country survived. The CDJ placed some 4,000 Jewish children and 10,000 adults in hiding, and 3,000 of the children survived.

There were about 3,000 Jews in **Luxembourg**. About a third of them escaped in advance of the invaders and then during the occupation the majority escaped to Vichy France and Portugal. About 800 Jews were deported but about 400 survived in Luxembourg. Although Jews had enjoyed complete freedom pre-war, when the occupation came some pro-Nazis emerged to persecute them.

There were some 140,000 Jews in the **Netherlands**, the majority of them Dutch citizens. About 25,000 were refugees from Germany, Austria and Poland. Due to high unemployment there was some resentment among the Dutch over the incomers so it was decided to establish in December 1938 a camp at Westerbork for the incomers rather than give them permanent residency. This was later used as a transit camp by the Germans.

The occupied country was ruled as a protectorate under a Reichscommissar and there was a strong SS presence looking after security. The most senior civil servants, the Secretaries-General, collaborated with the Germans in the belief that they could lessen the harshness of foreign rule. Only one senior civil servant resigned when civil servants had to declare whether they were Aryan, at the same time warning his colleagues of the consequences of conforming to German directives. The efficiency of the Dutch civil service unfortunately contributed to the high proportion of Jews who were deported from Holland. One Dutch civil servant even devised an ID card that was almost incapable of being reproduced effectively and this had widespread repercussions for Jews and opposition; although not a Nazi he went to Berlin to show it to the Gestapo; this devotion to duty caused immense problems for the underground. Another factor in the fate of the Dutch Jews was the difficulty in escaping to forested areas as little forest existed in the country; also the numerous canals and dykes meant that areas could be isolated easily by the occupiers. Jews were also concentrated as 60% resided in Amsterdam and this also aided the Germans. Although Holland was noted for its tolerance the Dutch Nazis were also strong with 80,000 members who were enthusiastic in seeking out Jews.

In November 1940 Jewish civil servants and university teachers were dismissed. In response, students at Leyden University and the Polytechnic School in Delft went on strike and teachers signed petitions for the reinstatement of their Jewish colleagues. The Germans responded by closing both universities. Dutch clergy spoke out against the regime in their churches and in November 1940 there was a non-public letter of protest against the banning of Jews from certain professions. In February 1941 Dutch SA men forced hotels and restaurants to put up 'No Jews Admitted' signs. But when Himmler ordered the round-up of Jews in Amsterdam in the same month, strikes in transport and industry, led by Communists, brought the city to a stand-still for three days. Strikes and demonstrations also took place in other cities although they were unfortunately followed by increased repression, seven strikers being killed and 100 leaders imprisoned.

The regime imposed a Jewish Council after clashes between Jews and Dutch Nazis and expected it to keep order in Jewish areas. The Council used its newspaper, *The Jewish Weekly*, to convey the Germans' anti-Jewish regulations. Permits for supposedly essential jobs were issued by the Jewish Council so that those holding them were exempt from deportation but the number of permits was gradually reduced to zero. The existence of the permits divided the community as they scrambled for the limited number. Jews were selected to administer Westerbork including drawing up of lists for deportation. President of the Supreme Court, L E Visser who was Jewish, was removed from his post and he strongly objected to the Jewish Council's collaboration with the Germans; however he died suddenly at the beginning of 1942. In May 1942 when a professor of law was dismissed 80% of the staff resigned.

When the first deportations of Jews began on 21 February 1942 Amsterdam shipyard workers went on strike. When the yellow star was made compulsory in spring of 1942 many non-Jewish people wore it too or wore yellow flowers. The Germans took action against this.

Once the deportations began most Jews did not present themselves at Westerbork and so the Germans had to send out special squads to find them. Some escaped from the country at this point with the help of escape networks, the most notable being Hechalutz which smuggled out hundreds of Jews. Others were hidden in the Netherlands itself and others still joined the resistance.

Protestant and Catholic churches protested about the dismissal of Jews from certain professions but this was not done publicly initially. In January 1941 RC Bishops had forbidden priests to give the sacraments to Nazis. Catholic and Protestant churches established relief funds. In February 1942 a three man delegation from Protestant and Catholic Churches met with Reichskommissar Arthur Seyss-Inquart to protest at the violation of three principles – 'justice, humanity and freedom of conscience'. In April an anti-Nazi proclamation was issued. When the deportation of baptised Jews was announced in 1942 the RC Church publicly protested and the regime responded by arresting Jewish Catholics and sending 100 to Auschwitz.

Late in 1942 the Welfare Organisation for Those in Hiding (LO) which was founded by a Calvinist minister and a housewife, became a mass movement. The following year it linked up with Catholic aid organisations. More than 1,000 of the LO lost their lives during the occupation. The organisation had about 15,000 volunteers and in the summer of 1944 they supplied 220,000 ration cards. Action groups mounted large scale raids on offices during 1943 to obtain ration cards, identity cards and stamps and seals. Documents that might have helped the police were also destroyed. Sometimes the raiders dressed as German servicemen or Dutch

Nazi Party members. When the founder of the LO was captured it was decided that his release would be attempted by a raid on the jail at Arnhem in June 1944. Not only was he released, so were fifty other prisoners, but another 150 refused to escape because of the fear of reprisals to others.

Sheltering of Jews was widespread, about 20-25,000, but nevertheless about 100,000 Jews were eliminated by the Nazis, mostly by deportation to Sobibor. More than half of those who were hidden survived.

The large proportion of Jews sent to their death in comparison with Belgium and France was partly due to rule by Nazis officials rather than the Wehrmacht. The Dutch administration was also very cooperative. When the Dutch police chief in Amsterdam, Tulp, ordered the round up of Jews in the summer of 1942 only one officer refused. Dutch railway workers also cooperated with the Government. The Government-in-Exile did not explicitly prohibit civil servants from carrying out anti-Jewish decrees until May 1943.

A general strike by Dutch workers took place in April-May 1943 to prevent the forced labour of Jews and non-Jews and as a consequence many deportations were prevented. However when a small Jewish resistance group killed a Nazi the Germans retaliated by sending 400 Jewish men and boys to Buchenwald. This provoked a strike by Dutch workers in several cities which lasted two days before being violently suppressed.

The village of Nieuwlande hid 120 Jewish children from Amsterdam. Albert Douwes, the son of the local pastor, brought the children there and arranged for farmers to take them in. All the children survived and many later went to Israel. Everyone participated and post-war the whole village was designated Righteous Among the Nations, the only other village recognised in this way being Le Chambon in France.

12,000 Jews were married to Dutch non-Jews and while the Germans put them into work-camps they did not deport them to avoid an outcry by the wider population. A German official, Hans Georg Calmeyer, certified many Jews as Aryan when they applied for reclassification and helped to save about 3,000 by this means.

Finland was a more fortunate location for Jews in spite of being an ally of Germany. Most Jews were refugees from Germany and Austria. Eight Jews were deported but when Himmler tried to pressure its Government to deport the remainder of around 2,000 he was rebuffed. Clergy protested as did members of the Social Democratic Party (a minority Party) and then the Government which had earlier agreed to Himmler's demands changed its stance and refused any further deportations. Thus all were saved.

Another German ally, **Italy**, was not in general anti-Semitic but Hitler pressured Mussolini to enact anti-Jewish legislation as early as 1933 although officials often did not enforce them. Prior to that a significant number of Jews had joined the Fascist Party. Although from 1939 the 50,000 Italian Jews were discriminated against – for example, they were excluded from the civl service and property ownership was restricted – they were not in danger of deportation. Foreign Jews were asked to leave Italy by March 1939 but this, like other legislation, was lax in its implementation. Moreover when Vichy France was taken over by Germany in November 1942 the Italians occupied eight French Departments which then became a place of refuge for French Jews. The Italians refused to hand over Jews to the Germans or to Vichy French. In Croatia Italian troops also intervened to save Jews and Serbs from being massacred by the extreme nationalist Ustase in the summer of 1941 and a few weeks later the protection of Croatian Jews was made official policy. Lieutenant Salvatore Loi with a corporal and two privates saved 400 Serbs who were about to be killed by Ustase. They also protected a fleeing column of Serbs and Jews.

However when northern Italy was occupied by Germany in September 1943 Italian Jews became endangered although the Italians generally obstructed attempts to deport them. But those in the French departments that had been occupied by the Italians were arrested and deported. Fr Marie-Benoit, who changed his name to Benedetto, worked in Rome with the Jewish relief agency who helped 4,000 Jews. There were around 8,000 Jews in Rome in danger but they were warned of the intended arrests and as a result some 7,000 escaped with the aid of Italians. Monsignor Alois Hudal, titular bishop of the German community in Rome, held anti-Semitic views and later helped Nazis with false papers to escape, but in spite of this when he was informed of the intended round-up of Jews in Rome he wrote to the German commander to try to stop the action.

In Secchiano in central Italy its 600 citizens helped Wolf and Esther Fullenbaum and their four-year-old daughter Carlotte for more than a year. They were housed in the second floor of a schoolhouse. If a search was imminent they were taken to the fields to blend in with the workers. The village priest was arrested and deported but the family was not discovered. In Assisi, immigrant Jews were sheltered in monasteries, convents and churches by the priests, nuns and bishops of the town. They were fortunate in that the German commander turned a blind eye and as a result between 100 and 200 were saved in spite of the Gestapo presence in the town. [See later The People of Assisi]

A well known sportsman, the cyclist Gino Bartali, secretly helped Jews. The most famous cyclist in Italy was also a devout Catholic who was a three-time winner of the Giro d'Italia before the war and also won the Tour de France in 1938. He hid a Jewish family in a house he owned and when asked by the Cardinal Archbishop of Florence to help in a rescuing network he used his bicycle to transport documents hidden in the frame and used his training schedule as a means of travelling around Tuscany between safe houses.

In 1944, 35,000 Jews were arrested by the Germans, helped by extreme fascist Italians, and put in camps near the Austrian border; of these 7,500 were sent to Auschwitz where most were killed, although this amounted to 15% of the Jewish population of Italy, one of the lowest of the occupied countries.

Albania had a very small Jewish population of 300 between the wars. In February 1939 100 refugees arrived from Vienna and were allowed to stay, then 300 more refugees in March were given permission. When the Italians invaded in April the government was replaced by a puppet government and the expulsion of all foreign Jews was demanded. However it was refused. When Italy surrendered to the Allies in July 1943 German troops occupied the country and asked for a list of all Jews this was refused and Albanian citizens, Christian and Muslim, began to hide the Jews. This was an expression of a traditional custom that a person who asks for your help is treated as an honoured guest to be protected. Thus the great majority of Jews in the country were saved.

Pre-war **Romania** was the most anti-Semitic state in Europe. At the end of the First World War the Allies pressured Romania to grant its Jews citizenship but these concessions were withdrawn in 1937 thus it became the second country to establish an anti-Semitic regime. There were about 850,000 Jews at the beginning of the Second World War. A strong Fascist movement called the Iron Guard developed. Fascist groups instigated pogroms and when Marshal Ion Antonescu took power in September 1940 a period of terror led by the Iron Guard broke out. Early in 1941 fighting between the army and the Iron Guard led to Antonescu taking dictatorial control using the army. The army also committed atrocities and used concentration camps as well as massacres. It instituted the practice of Jews being herded into railcars and sent through the countryside without any aim. Ironically the Germans were horrified at the disorganised nature of their slaughter. In February 1941 Romania entered the war as an ally of Germany. The next year Eichmann prepared to transport 200,000 Romanian Jews to death camps at Lublin in Poland. It was only then that some opposition arose and well known intellectual, political and religious figures spoke out. At this point Antonescu refused to comply to German demands and authorised Jews to emigrate to Palestine in return for payment for although anti-Semitic the Romanian regime was also corrupt. In 1943 the Government contacted the Allies and prepared to change sides. As the Red Army approached the killing was stopped and Jews were released even without payment. More than half of Romania's Jews thus survived.

One deeply concerned official was the mayor of Czernowitz, Dr Traian Popovici, who objected to the establishment of a ghetto in the city and also wrote to his superiors about a planned deportation of local Jews pointing out that they had made a great contribution to the economic and cultural life of Romania. Eventually about 20,000 mostly professional Jews were exempted as a result of his efforts. The mayor added other names to the list of those who came to see him at great risk to himself.

The Queen Mother of Romania, Queen Elena, also made strenuous efforts to save Jews and was successful in some instances.

During an outbreak of anti-Semitism by Romanians a group of 5,000 Jews were packed into cattle trucks on a train without food or water. They were kept on the train for 8 days shunting from station to station pointlessly. At Roman station one woman, head of the regional Red Cross, Viorica Agarici, insisted on the German guards opening the doors so that food and water could be given and 1,000 of them were actually allowed off the train and most of these survived. Of those 4,000 who remained on the train more than half were dead by the time it was decided to end the ordeal.

Bulgaria, unlike most of eastern Europe, displayed little anti-Semitism. The 50,000 Jews had legal equality with non-Jews and were integrated economically but maintained separate schools. The fascist movement was small. However in February 1940 King Boris III, who had substantial political power, and prime minister Bogdan Filov introduced relatively moderate anti-Jewish legislation which had many exemptions, such as all baptised Jews, a regulation which led to many new Christian converts. The proposed law provoked protests from the Orthodox Church and various intellectuals but it was nevertheless passed by the parliament in January 1941. Bulgaria then entered the war on Germany's side and parts of Greece, Yugoslavia and Romania were given to Bulgaria.

Under pressure from Germany Jews were deported to the countryside but this dispersion of people only made action against them more difficult. In August 1942 crowds tried to stop Jews being ordered to the railway station in Sophia and they went on to demonstrate outside the Palace. 350 Jews also protested at the Ministry of the Interior and the Minister met them in person. In September 1942 the Yellow Star was made compulsory, although the Bulgarians produced a very small Star, but this was followed by a critical sermon on 27 September by Metropolitan Stephan of Sophia. In October the government asked the press to stop attacks on Jews and they also stopped production of Yellow Stars.

In January 1943 Theodor Dannecker, assistant to Eichmann, was sent from Berlin to Sofia to see the Minister for Jewish Affairs, the anti-Semitic Aleksandur Belev, to get things moving. This was effective and 20,000 foreign Jews were deported to Treblinka followed by another 12,000 in March. More than 4,000 Bulgarian Jews were also arrested which led to opposition within the parliament, and Bishop Kiril threatened to launch civil disobedience and even lie down on the rail track himself to stop the trains. The former Attorney General led a protest in Parliament and lawyers, doctors, writers and communists joined the opposition. Metropolitan Stephan gave protection to the Chief Rabbi of Sophia. The order to deport was postponed. Angelo Roncalli, later Pope John XXIII, in Turkey also interceded with King Boris, and he asked the Turkish Government to protect Jews who reached Turkey and also tried to stop the deportation of Jews from Salonica although without success. The King eventually cancelled the order.

After the battle of Stalingrad King Boris determined to prevent deportations but accepted the German idea of assigning Jews to road building in the countryside. Hundreds of Jews protested in Sofia on 24 May 1943 and went on to the Royal Palace where they were stopped by the police. Various groups such as Christians and Communists appealed to the Jews not to leave the capital. When Metropolitan Stefan heard of it he telephoned the Palace and then walked to the public celebration at which all Government Ministers were present and appealed to them. Prime Minister Filov told Stefan not to interfere in politics but Stefan wrote a long letter to the King demanding cancellation of the deportation and all the bishops supported him. The order was rescinded. In August King Boris died in mysterious circumstances but the situation of the Jews did not improve for the Nazis. The German representatives in Bulgaria itself realised the situation was hopeless.

In the summer of 1944 the Bulgarian minister of Istanbul started negotiations with the US War Refugee Board about evacuating the Jews to Palestine through Turkey. On 24 August discrimination against Jews in Bulgaria was abolished. Shortly afterwards the Russian army entered Bulgaria. Thus nearly all the Jews with Bulgarian citizenship survived.

In **Serbia** partisan warfare against the Germans was used as an excuse to kill Jews and thousands of men were shot by the Wehrmacht while the women and children were gassed in vans by the German security police. About 5,000 Jews joined the partisans.

In **Croatia** about 95% of the Jews, some 30,000, were deported by the fascist Ustashe who were also staunch Catholics. The Croats carried out the deportations and paid the Germans 30 marks for each Jew while in return the Croats kept the property of those deported. However 5% of Jews (1500) were assimilated and the Croatian elite often married Jewish women and that minority survived. But in Croatia it was those of the Orthodox faith (as well as Roma) who suffered in much greater numbers, close to half a million Orthodox Serbs have been estimated to have been slaughtered by Catholics including Franciscan priests. The failure of Pope Pius XII to condemn and take action against the genocidal actions of the Catholic Ustashe is astounding.

A Croat Catholic woman, Mathilda Nitsch, who had a boarding house in Susak on the Adriatic coast sheltered Jews in her boarding house and then took them to friends in Fiume where at night they were put on boats which took them to other parts of Italy. She was discovered by the Italian Secret Police who interrogated her with torture but she did not reveal her helpers.

Greece remained neutral on the outbreak of the war but Italy invaded it in October 1940. When the Italians were driven back Germany came to Italy's help. The north of Greece was occupied by the Germans and the south by the Italians. Salonica had a large population of mainly Sephardic Jews, about 55,000, and they were nearly all deported. Their only hope of escape was to flee south.

When the Italian army collapsed the Germans rounded up all Jews they could find. Most Greeks were indifferent to the plight of the Jews but some were helped by being hidden in monasteries and convents on the instruction of Archbishop Papandreou Damaskinos. Also the Chief of Police for Athens, Angelos Evert, issued false documents for Jews.

Zakinthos island had 275 Jews in 1939 and until 1943 it was under Italian occupation but on 9 September 1943 a German force landed on the island and the mayor was ordered to draw up a list of Jews. The mayor consulted the Metropolitan Chrysostomos who said he would negotiate with the Germans and told the mayor to destroy the list. The Germans insisted on seeing the list so Chrysostomos wrote his name on a paper and handed it over saying "There is the list of Jews requested". He then alerted the Jews and urged them to go into hiding in the mountains. Two-thirds did so and were supplied with essentials by the islanders. In August 1944 three small German boats arrived to remove the Jews but they could not find any.

Many Greek Jews operated the gas chambers in the extermination camps. When liberation was near those in Auschwitz revolted but were wiped out, except for one person. Only about 15,000 Jews out of a population of 75,000 survived.

With its very large Jewish population (3,300,000) **Poland** saw much rescue work by the Christian population even although in the end Polish Jews were the largest nationality among those eliminated. Jews formed a tenth of the total Polish population and a quarter of the urban population. Life became increasingly difficult for them during the 1930s with anti-Semitic legislation enacted in a country with a long tradition of prejudice against Jews. Following the creation of modern Poland at the end of the First World War the new government was required to guarantee equality for minorities, a requirement that was widely resented. When the Germans occupied the country the rural Jews were forced into the cities and then all Jews into ghettos. A particular disadvantage the Jews of Poland faced was that the majority were distinct from the Christian Poles, in appearance and in culture. Yiddish was the first language of the majority with only 12% giving Polish as their native language and they had built organisations that were specifically Jewish. The assimilated Jews, unlike those in Western Europe, were a minority.

The Warsaw ghetto was established in November 1940 and its population eventually reached about 400,000 producing extreme over-crowding. About 2,400 stayed out of the ghetto and were able to live as non-Jews due to being acculturated; many were Christian converts. From the beginning only 10% of necessities was supplied to the ghetto and so smuggling developed and these routes were later important for escape. Until mid-1941 the Poles fought Russia as well as Germany and when many Jews fled to the Russian zone it confirmed the belief of many Poles that Jews were pro-Communist as Jews were already members of the Polish Communist Party in greater proportion than non-Jews. In October 1941 it was announced that Poles hiding Jews would themselves be executed.

From late 1941 the Germans established extermination camps for Jews at Chelmno, Auschwitz, Belzec, Majdanek, Sobibor and Treblinka which were to deal with Jews from the West as well as Poland. The number of Polish Jews killed by various means was to reach three million before the end of the War. On 22 July 1942 the Judenrat, or Jewish Council, was informed that "all Jewish persons living in Warsaw will be resettled in the East". This was the start of the Great Deportation or first Aktion and by 12 September 270,000 Jews had been killed.

The Polish Blue Police (those police now under German command) helped the occupiers in supervision of the ghettos and hunting down escaped Jews. Some factions of the Polish Home Army (Armia Krajova or AK) sometimes fought Jewish partisan groups or refused to accept Jews as members of their fighting groups.

There were other Poles who helped Jews including those in Zegota, the Council for Aid to Jews. This had been formed in late 1942 by Catholic intellectuals and others of left political persuasion. Its work was funded by the Government-in-Exile as well as foreign Jewish organisations and they placed Jews in hiding and supplied them with essentials. They also tried to stop informers and blackmailers but its work did not start until the end of 1942 which was too late for the majority of Jews.

Some opposition to Jewish persecution came from the RC Church but was mainly concerning the fate of Christians of Jewish origin. Letters from the Polish bishops to Rome rarely mention the Jews, in contrast to bishops in other countries. An exception was the Bishop of Pinsk who worked with underground organisations that had links with the ghetto. In contrast to the Church hierarchy, from mid-1942 especially many clergy helped Jews, particularly children. About 7,000 Jewish children were hidden, mostly with Catholic families and about 500 were in convents and 700 in orphanages. Out of 10,017 priests 1,811 were killed by the Germans.

Zegota tried to rescue Jewish children by placing them in homes, convents and orphanages. However even among rescuers anti-Semitic views were sometimes present. This was true of Zegota's founder, the writer and underground resister Zofia Kossak-Szczucka, who nevertheless opposed killing because of her Christian beliefs. Zegota had Jews on its Board and it forged documents and found safe houses, and medical care was provided by physicians who were members of the underground. It was active from December 1942 till the liberation. Kossak-Szczucka was arrested and sent to Auschwitz concentration camp but was later released and survived the war.

Paulsson estimates that about 17,000 Jews in hiding in Warsaw were helped by 70-90,000 people or one-twelfth of the non-Jewish population. About 11,500 of those in hiding survived.

(See Irena Sendlerova and other Polish Rescuers)

Czechoslovakia which was taken over in March 1939 was a strongly Catholic country. During the republican period between the First and Second World Wars a Slovak People's Party was founded by a RC priest which became similar to the German Nazi Party. In 1938 Msgr Josef Tiso became leader of the Party, then became Prime Minister and finally President of the puppet state, in spite of Pope Pius XII being opposed to the principle of a priest as head of government. A Jewish Codex was introduced on 9 September 1941. Because of the strength of Catholicism baptised Jews were given favoured treatment. However Deputy Protector Heydrich persuaded the Government led by Tiso to abolish the distinction between baptised and non-baptised Jews. The Vatican Secretary of State condemned this legislation. A ghetto was established at Terezin or Theresienstadt (in German) serving as both a showplace camp and also as a staging post for Auschwitz.

In March 1942 five collection points were set up for deportation. The first transport contained 999 young women destined for Auschwitz. By October about 60,000 Jews had been deported. Jewish leaders protested and they contacted religious leaders including the Papal Nuncio in Budapest, Msgr Angelo Rotta, who informed the Vatican. Deportations were then stopped. However both Catholic and Protestant leaders were concerned mainly for baptised Jews and most of the population was indifferent to the fate of Jews in general. Nevertheless individual priests, including the bishop of Presov, spoke out for the Jews.

Early in 1943 it appeared that deportations would be resumed and Jewish organisations launched protests. Their appeal reached the Papal Nuncio in Istanbul, Msgr Angelo Roncalli (later Pope John XXIII), and he made representations to the Vatican. The Apostolic Delegate in Bratislava, Msgr Guiseppi Burzio, then met Prime Minister Tuka in April and warned of the possible consequences post-war. With the war going badly for the German forces on the eastern front a revolt was called by the Slovakian underground but it was suppressed and round-ups were restarted. Between October 1944 and March 1945, about 13,000 Jews were deported.

A rescuer, Zdenek Urbanek, who posted food parcels to Terazin, took a family of three into his Prague apartment but after three weeks they got the opportunity of moving to a farm in Bohemia and they survived the war. In the town of Eger where the 1,800 Jews were confined to a ghetto the local bishop, Czapik Gyula, forbade the priests to assist in the deportations in any way and in June 1944 during the round-up he saved eight women by giving them jobs in his kitchen. Premysl Pitter, head of a home for abandoned children, used to send milk regularly to a Jewish orphanage and he collected food and sent it to concentration camps and to Jewish families. He hid some children in his institution and when investigated by the Gestapo he and his assistant Olga Fierrz smuggled them to a children's home in a village. About 100 were saved in this way.

Out of a Jewish population of some 250,000 only about 50,000 survived.

After the fall of the **Danish** Government in 1943 the Germans stole the files on Jews in Copenhagen. The Chief Rabbi and his son were arrested on 31 August and on 18 September Hitler ordered the deportation of Jews. There were widespread protests from the churches and professional bodies. The Lutheran Bishop Fuglsang-Damgaard issued a proclamation affirming the need to defend the freedom of the Jews. The head of the German administration, Werner Best, asked for Wehrmacht men as he could not rely on Danish police but the commander General von Hannechen refused to cooperate as he disagreed with Best's relatively lenient approach to governing Denmark and so police had to be brought from Germany. The Attaché at the German Embassy, Georg F Duckwitz, tried to persuade Best to abandon his plans and then went to Sweden to ask them to intervene diplomatically, which they did but without effect. On 28 September, Duckwitz warned the Danish resistance of plans of the round up of 1-2 October. On 29 September the Rabbi of Copenhagen warned his people. The result was that on the morning of 2 October, only 475 Jews were arrested out of 7,695 in Denmark. They were deported to Theresienstadt. Other Jews were hidden and then ferried to Sweden by fisherman who were paid. Some Danish police took part in the rescue. Of the 475 only 111 did not return. It was the most successful of the rescue operations in Europe. [See Denmark – national rescue of Jews 1940-45]

The number of Jews in **Norway** was even smaller than in Denmark, about 1,700 of whom about 200 were Germans and Austrians who had fled from their homeland since 1933. In April 1941 the synagogue in Trondheim was vandalised by local anti-Semites. The leading clergyman in the city warned the local Nazis that persecution of the Jews would not be tolerated. The leading Methodist offered the Jews his church attic for their services, but advised them to enter and leave discretely. In February 1942 all seven bishops of the Lutheran Church resigned in protest at Jewish policy.

On 25 October 1942 Sigrid Lund received a mysterious non-explicit phone call which she guessed was a warning that Jews were about to be rounded up. She and a friend (an English woman Myrtle Wright) tried to contact as many Jews as possible without using the telephone. For some it was too late as they had already been picked up and some others did not believe the warning. In November most of the churches protested publicly about the roundup.

On 25 November the administrator of the Jewish Children's Home in Oslo received a warning that the children and staff were going to be arrested. She contacted members of the resistance who managed to get the children to a villa in the suburbs from where they were later taken to safety in Sweden.

The first deportation to Auschwitz took place on the night of 26-27 November 1942 when 523 Jews were taken by ship and then by train to Stettin. Many Norwegians gathered at the quayside but found they were unable to help. As well as private homes, a number of hospitals were used to hide Jews until they could be smuggled across the border into Sweden. Among the smugglers was Odd Nansen, son of the famous explorer and humanitarian Fridjof Nansen. Odd Nansen was arrested by the Gestapo and sent to Sachsenhausen concentration camp but survived the war. On the night of 3 December, forty Jews including Henriette Samuel, the wife of the Chief Rabbi of Norway, and her children, were packed into two trucks supposedly carrying potatoes and when the trucks could take them no further they all walked in minus-twenty degree temperatures to the Swedish border. About 800 Jews in total were brought to safety by this means.

Those Jews who were deported to Germany, more than 700, were nearly all killed.

In **Germany** a boycott of Jewish businesses was called by the Government in April 1933, only three months after Hitler became Chancellor, and was generally adhered to by the German population, which did not bode well for anti-Nazis and Jews. The same year saw the removal of Jews from the civil service, which included teachers in schools and universities, and was also met with little opposition. In 1933 there were about half a million Jews in Germany; more than 100,000 emigrated before the end of 1938 and emigration accelerated after 9-10 November 1938 when Jewish premisses including synagogues were attacked, the episode known as Kristallnacht. Thus about half of the Jewish population had left by the start of the war. Austria, which had about 180,000 Jews, saw an even larger exodus.

After the Nuremberg Laws were enacted in 1935 (a Jew being defined as having at least one Jewish grandparent) the Catholic Church tried to protect Christians of Jewish descent and assisted them to emigrate. When the Star of David was made compulsory, Berlin bishops Wienken and Berning tried to get an exemption for converted Jews but this was denied them.

Kristallnacht, the attack on Jews and their property by Hitler's SA which had been sparked by the assassination of a German embassy official in Paris, was a turning point in the persecution of the Jews. However it was not universally popular among the German population and many thought that matters had gone too far. Following Kristallknacht, Provost Bernhard Lichtenberg of St Hedwig's Cathedral, Berlin, led his congregation in prayers for Jews and then offered prayers every evening for prisoners until arrested in 1941. He had earlier led demonstrations outside concentration camps. He died on the way to Dachau in 1943. On Kristallnacht, Cardinal Faulhaben sent a truck to the Chief Rabbi of Munich to help salvage sacred relics. In Schnaittach in Franconia, the synagogue was set on fire but the head of the local history museum, Gottfried Stammler, ordered the fire brigade to put out the fire.

He was then threatened with being sent to Dachau by a local Nazi but responded that the building was valuable and was supported in this by the Mayor. The fire was extinguished although there was damage. He then collected Thora scrolls from this synagogue and others in the region and hid them under the floorboards of the museum. At the end of the war he handed them over to the remnants of the Jewish community.

Bishop Konrad von Preysing of Berlin had expressed the view that Nazi and Christian beliefs were totally incompatible and in November 1942 preached on the right of all people to life. In December 1942 Bishop Josef Frings wrote a pastoral letter for the diocese of Cologne opposing violation of the rights of all people. Jesuit Father Rupert Mayer, who had been awarded an Iron Cross as a Chaplain in the First World War and had lost a leg, became active in anti-Nazi workers' groups and was imprisoned for six months in 1937 for preaching against anti-Semitism. He was later sent to Sachsenhausen and then spent the war under house arrest in a Benedictine monastery.

Shortly before the war started groups organised the production of false documents and one group in Stuttgart was led by 19-year-old Marion Fuerst, who was tall and had fair hair which gave her some protection. She worked in a department store where during the day she slipped forged documents and money to Jewish customers who whispered a code word for that day.

Pastor Heinrich Grüber of the Confessing Church decided to work full time helping Christians of Jewish origin and built up a staff of 35 who worked from the Buro Grüber, as it was called, in Berlin starting in 1935. They worked closely with German Quakers. The main work was organising escape routes to the Netherlands. In December 1940 Grüber attempted to go to the Gurs concentration camp in Vichy France where German Jews had been sent and were living in very poor conditions. With the help of anti-Nazi Germans he was able to get medicines, money and other essentials to the camp. But before he reached Camp de Gurs he was arrested and sent to Sachsenhausen concentration camp and then Dachau but after a heart attack he was released in 1943. He survived the war but eight of his staff did not. In contrast, many Christians gave active support to the new regime and only about 50 pastors out of 17,000 in Germany received substantial prison sentences.

Many individual pastors and priests and nuns actively protected Jews but the churches as institutions were weak in their defence. They gave higher priority to defending their own faith and institutions.

Baptists, Methodists, Mormons, Adventists all discriminated against Jews in Germany with only the Quakers and Jehovah's Witnesses being consistent in their defence. Jehovah's Witnesses were the staunchest opponents of the regime. There were around 20,000 in the country and they were imprisoned in labour camps from 1935 onwards. They refused any compromise and by 1945 were spread around all the concentration camps in occupied Europe. Witness children were often taken from their parents to be brought up in Nazi homes. The majority of Christians, whether Catholic or Protestant, either supported the regime or didn't actively oppose it.

A construction engineer, Hermann Graebe, who supervised construction of railroads in the Ukraine, Poland and Germany recruited Jewish labour in order to protect them (like Oskar Schindler in Poland) and he saved more than 300 people this way. Sadly after the war he was ostracised and his actions criticised by other Germans to the extent that he emigrated to the USA.

In Berlin in March 1943 the remaining Jews, who were men married to non-Jewish women, were rounded up and imprisoned in a building in the Rosenstrasse with the intention of transporting them to their deaths. Some 6,000 people (1,700 of them were wives of the imprisoned) gathered and demanded the release of the men. This went on for a week and in spite of the Gestapo HQ nearby they did not act against the women fearing that the protests might spread. Goebbels and Himmler ordered the men's release.

In May such Jews as were in camps in Germany were exempted from deportation in order to avoid similar demonstrations. [See under Case Studies]

An unusual rescuer was the brother of Hermann Goering, Albert Goering. Albert did not follow Hermann into the Nazi party and indeed was opposed to what it stood for. On many occasions he intervened to protect individuals by using the power of the Goering name. However this required that Hermann give backing to his brother's interventions, or at the very least give tacit support, which surprisingly he did. Albert on the other hand had to pretend that he was on the side of the regime, although the Gestapo had a file on him. His actions led to the survival of dozens of Jews and others. After the war he was arrested by the Allies and spent about two years in prison but was eventually cleared by the intervention of some of those he had protected.

Another rescuer was unusual in that he was a Muslim. Mohamed Helmy was born in Khartoum in 1901, his parents being Egyptian. He went to Berlin in 1922 to study medicine and after qualifying obtained a post at the Robert Koch Institute but he was dismissed from that in 1937 as a non-Aryan. He was also unable to marry his German fiancée because of the race laws and he and other Egyptians were arrested in 1939 but he was released after a year because of ill-health. He then hid a Jewish friend, 21-year-old Anna Boros who was in danger of deportation, in a cabin he used in the outskirts of Berlin from March 1942 till the end of the war. She was sometimes moved to other friends' houses when he was interrogated. He also helped to hide Anna's mother, step father and grandmother. After the war he was able to marry his fiancée. He died in 1982 and was recognised as a Righteous Gentile in 2013, being the first Muslim to be so.

Kurt Gerstein, who came from a conservative patriotic family and whose father was a judge, joined the Nazi Party but also joined the Protestant Confessing Church and as a result was expelled from the Party and spent some time in prison in the late 1930s. In spite of this he managed to join the SS in 1941 and became useful to the extermination programme as an engineer. He witnessed mass murders in Belzac and Treblinka camps and attempted to convey this knowledge to the Allies through a Swedish diplomat and other contacts including the Vatican. He became responsible for ordering prussic acid which is essential for the manufacture of Xyklon-B gas which was used in the gas chambers but claimed he did his best to sabotage production. At the end of the war he wrote the Gerstein Report which in part exaggerated the scale of the extermination but was in essence true. He was arrested by the French and imprisoned as a possible war criminal but he apparently committed suicide.

A case of resistance by German soldiers was in Slonim in Poland, when they were ordered to kill Jews there on 15 October 1941. Several soldiers refused to carry out the massacre and were merely ordered to groom and clean horses for two weeks as a punishment. Some of the Germans there also helped Jews to escape. [Kassow p.458, note 39]

Captain Wilm Hosenfeld of the Wehrmacht, who had been a teacher before the war and had joined the Nazi Party, became increasingly alienated by what he saw when stationed in Poland and consequently used his position to save a number of individual Poles, some of them Jewish. The best known was the pianist and composer Wladyslaw Szpilman whom he discovered hiding in a ruined building in Warsaw and brought food and other necessities to him. Szpilman survived to have a successful post-war career but Hosenfeld was imprisoned by the Russians. Hosenfeld kept a diary during the war in which he was scathing of the Nazi regime. Attempts by people rescued by him were made to secure his release after the war but this was unsuccessful and he died in a Russian prison.

A diplomat who was the rescuer of many **Austrian** Jews was Dr Feng Shan Ho. He was Consul-General for China in Vienna. In spite of the disapproval of his superior, the Ambassador in Berlin, he signed many visas to allow Jews to get out of Austria and go to

Shanghai. From there many went on to Hong Kong or Australia. By these means he must have saved several thousands of Jews. Although attempts to derail his career were made by the Germans and his own superiors he remained in the diplomatic service post-war.

One of many narrow escapes was of a young Jewish woman called Erika. In 1942 she was given shelter in the Vienna flat of Dr Ella Lingens-Reiner. A couple of teacher friends obtained the necessary ration cards for her but when Erika needed surgery for appendicitis it was the maid of the house who offered her papers so that Erika could get admitted to hospital. Later Erika decided one day to sunbathe on the roof of the building but was spotted by neighbours on a building opposite who contacted the police. A policeman called at the flat but Erika did not open it. Knowing that someone was inside he shouted that he would go to fetch someone to open the door. A short time later the door was opened from the outside – it was a girlfriend of Lingens-Reiner's brother-in-law who had a key. The situation was quickly explained to her so that when the policeman reappeared the girlfriend opened the door and said she had not opened it the first time as she was ashamed to have been seen naked.

Helena Horowitz escaped from the ghetto of the Polish town of Debica in December 1942. Although she had no papers she managed to get a job in another town working for a Viennese construction firm. There an overseer called Lambert Grutsch, who knew she was Jewish, offered to get her out of Poland. He applied for permission for her to serve as a maid and farmhand for his wife. When he was going home for a vacation to the Austrian Tyrol in February 1944 he took her officially as a slave-worker. In this remote valley she worked on the farm until liberation.

Sergeant Anton Schmidt, an Austrian conscript in the Wehrmacht, who was stationed in Vilnius, Lithuania, observed the round up of Jews and decided to help them. He supplied forged papers and managed to get Jews out of the ghetto and then using army trucks got them out of the city. By this means he rescued about 250 men, women and children before being arrested early in 1942 and executed. He had been warned by the Jewish underground that he was in danger but he felt compelled to continue as long as he could.

In 1938 anti-Jewish legislation was enacted in **Hungary** which had about 400,000 Jews. There was a strong Fascist movement called the Arrow Cross. Here as in many countries there was a clear distinction made between Hungarian and foreign Jews. 130,000 Hungarian Jews were enrolled in the army and sent to fight on the eastern front. But in August 1941 18,000 foreign Jews were deported to the Ukraine and 16,000 were massacred. Political power moved during the war between different factions in Hungary and between Hungary and Germany and the fortunes of the Jewish population swung back and forth. Nicholas Kallay's 1942 regime was relatively moderate and he got Admiral Horthy, the regent, to resist German demands to deport 100,000 Jews. But Kallay was forced to resign in March 1944 and Hungarian police then began large scale deportations.

A remarkable woman, Margit Slachta, was the first woman to be elected to the Hungarian Parliament, in 1920. She became a Benedictine nun and founded a Society of the Sisters of Social Service. From the beginning she openly attacked the persecution of the Jews. She published a newspaper, *Voice of the Spirit*, which was suppressed in 1943 but continued to be distributed through the underground. Slachta met the Pope in March 1943 to inform him of the Jewish situation. She instructed her convents to open their doors to Jews and her society supplied food, clothing and medicine in Budapest during the last months of the war. One of her Sisters was killed by the Arrow Cross and she herself was beaten up. When Germans came to inspect a children's convalescent home she boldly confronted them and did not allow them to speak to the children. She also obtained protective documents for an important religious leader, Aaron Rokeach, known as the Belzer Rebbe, whose whole family including seven children had been killed in Poland.

The Swede Raoul Wallenberg arrived in Budapest on 9 July 1944 with the specific task of rescuing Jews. At the Swedish Embassy he started issuing entry permits to the total of 15,000 eventually. The Legations of Switzerland, Spain and Portugal, the Red Cross, the Papal Nuncio, and Latin American Consuls also issued papers to Jews. Wallenburg also acquired food and used bluff, bribery and influence to save lives. Friedrich Born of the International Committee of the Red Cross claimed many buildings and hospitals as sovereign territory of the Red Cross and gave forged papers to those sheltering there. He established a Jewish Affairs Department within his office and hired 3,000 Jews to save them from deportation; another Red Cross employee complained but Born ignored him. He later visited the deportation camps set up by Eichmann to make a personal protest. When the Nazis took control of Hungary in October 1944 Auschwitz was no longer available so 50,000 Jews were marched towards Germany in November 1944 and treated with great brutality by the Arrow Cross. Himmler, seeing that the war was going badly, ordered the march to stop. Some 95,000 Jews survived in the ghettos and 25,000 in homes, churches and elsewhere. [See Case Studies]

The **Baltic countries**, like Poland, were often pawns of the Russian and German empires. In July 1940 they were occupied once more by the Russians and their harsh treatment of the occupants made them very unpopular so that when the Germans invaded these countries in June 1941 they were generally welcomed.

Lithuania had a high proportion of Jews – there were about 200,000 out of 3 million – with a vigorous cultural life. Rescuers were few and anti-Semitism had increased during the 1930s. The RC Primate would not intervene on behalf of the Jews in case it endangered the Catholic Church. In spite of the indifference of the hierarchy of the Church there were priests who protested against the persecution and who hid Jews. Only around a quarter of the Jews survived.

One rescuer was Ona Simaite, a librarian at the University of Vilna, who along with two other women founded a Committee to Rescue Jews. They found hiding places, forged documents and raised funds for hundreds of Jews. Simaite got permission to enter the ghetto to recover library books lent to Jews and she smuggled in food at the same time. In the summer of 1944 she adopted a ten-year-old Jewish girl registering her as a relative but the Germans discovered that it was untrue and she was tortured for information about hiding places but revealed nothing, then was sent to Dachau but she survived the war.

Elena Kutorgene was a medical doctor who helped Jews who had been her patients before the war but also others who came to her for help. Before the Germans arrived, rampaging mobs of Lithuanians sought out Jews to murder them and Elena sheltered several Jews in her surgery overnight. When the Kovno ghetto was created she took food and medicines there to hand through the fence.

In the ghetto of Vilna people with typhus were to be selected for extermination so doctors at the hospital falsified their medical records to keep them out of Nazi hands.

The Japanese consul in Kovno, Sempo Sugihara, issued a transit visa through Japan to a Dutch Jewish student who had obtained an entry permit from the Dutch consul for Curacao in Latin America. Permission to issue it was refused but he ignored the instructions. Many other Jews followed and he and his wife wrote as many visas as possible and when the legation was closed down by the Russians they operated from a hotel until they had to return to Japan. He three times defied instructions to stop. At least 4,500 Jews were thus saved. Sugihara lost his diplomatic career and was ostracised but later found a job with a trading company.

The record of **Latvia** was even worse that that of Lithuania. Out of some 80,000 Jews only about 3,000 were saved. But as everywhere there were individuals who were prepared to help. One rescuer was Janis Lipke who smuggled people out of the Riga ghetto and hid them in his house or in friends' homes. He and his wife and son built a hiding place under a shed. He got more than 50 people out of the ghetto but only about a dozen of these survived as some in the countryside were betrayed. Many neighbours after the war could not understand why they bothered to help Jews.

Amfian Gerasimov had an unhappy adolescence living at first with his father who had divorced his mother and remarried, and then with his mother in Moscow. Seeking for stability in his life he came in time to the view that Judaism was the foundation of all religions. He had married and moved to Riga and worked as a postman which enabled him to deliver messages and goods to Jews in the ghetto. Rich Jews asked him to keep their goods safe for them which he did and then delivered their possessions so that they could barter for food and favours in the ghetto. He thus was indirectly responsible for saving some lives. Long after the war he and his son settled in Israel.

Yanis Vabulis was a former army officer who worked in a construction company. He gave shelter to 21-year-old Zelda Shelshelovich who otherwise would have died in a terrible mass slaughter. He pretended that she was his girlfriend. When he entertained fellow army officers they would often boast of their participation in the slaughter of Jews which included Zelda's whole family. After the war Yanis and Zelda married.

Pauls Krumins was director of a music conservatory in Daugavpils. A former talented violin student, Cecilia Gradis, who was Jewish was in danger when the Germans invaded in June 1941. Her sister Nadya and she were imprisoned and their parents executed but the sisters were released and Krumins took them into his family home and obtained papers in Latvian names for them.

While in 1942 they were getting their papers renewed Nadya was recognised and they were arrested again but Krumins managed to get them released by passing them as his nieces and the two then went to Vilnius. Just after the sisters left Krumins was arrested by the Gestapo and imprisoned for eight months but the sisters survived to the end of the war mainly as slave labourers in Austria.

In **Estonia** there were only about 4,000 Jews and of these some 3,000 escaped to the USSR before the SS arrived to wipe out almost all those who remained. One of the few to survive in Estonia was Isidor Levin who was hidden by his Bible teacher Dr Uku Masing and his wife Eha.

Large numbers of Jews lived in the **Ukraine** and in **Byelorussia,** and in the USSR as a whole there were as many as 3-4 million Jews. As the Germans penetrated into Russian territory the Einsatzgruppen squads slaughtered on a huge scale. One of the most notorious episodes was at Babi Yar near Kiev where 33,000 Jews were shot in two days in 1941. (Later, even larger numbers of residents of the area of all ethnicities were massacred at the ravine at Babi Yar.)

In parts of the Ukraine there were Baptists with a particular respect for Jews and individual families often hid one or more Jews in spite of the general hostile environment. Individual Ukrainians, mostly in the countryside, would sometimes provide hiding places for Jews but other Ukrainian nationalists would willingly do the Nazis' murderous work for them.

When the Germans took over the town of Lotczk, the Jews were moved into the ghetto including a bank clerk, David Frital. When the Germans started killing ghetto Jews he escaped and ran to the home of a bank employee, Irena Bron, and asked for shelter for one night. The father, Zigmund Bron, agreed. In the morning Frital decided to make himself useful by lighting the fire and peeling potatoes and when Zigmund went off to work he did other chores around the house and looked after Zigmund's wife who had poor health. Thus one night extended to days and then weeks until Frital asked if he could stay through the winter and leave in the spring. The Brons were worried but relieved when they confided to their priest who gave his blessing. Frital left in May 1942 of his own accord.

In the Ukraine surprising opposition to killing of Jews came from the Metropolitan of the Unite Church, Andrej Szeptyckyj, for he was anti-Semitic and a Ukrainian nationalist and yet he opposed the killing of Jews and wrote protests to Himmler and the Pope; the latter counselled patience. The Metropolitan even sheltered Jews in monasteries and in his own residence.

In the Byelorussian capital, Minsk, a group of women smuggled children out of the ghetto and settled them in orphanages. Seventy children were saved by this means. Anna Dvach helped a Jewish woman with whom she had worked in a factory. She took her home and gave her food and sent her to the ghetto with food for others. By this means thirteen Jews survived until the Red Army arrived six months later.

Conscientious Objectors and Pacifist Resisters

Pacifists were high on the Nazi list of undesirables; those who refused to be conscripted into the army or who were outspoken in their opposition to the regime were severely dealt with. Soon after Hitler came to power in 1933 pacifist organisations were suppressed. Military conscription was reinstated in 1935. The number of conscientious objectors (COs) in Germany probably only amounted to a few hundred, the majority being Jehovah's Witnesses. When Buchenwald was liberated around 300 JWs were found who had been there from the establishment of the camp eight years previously; others had been shot. A break away group from the Seventh-day Adventists known as the Reformation Movement, consisting of about 500 members, adhered to the traditional position of not taking up arms; at least four of them were shot.

Today the best known conscientious objector from that period is Franz Jägerstätter, an Austrian farmer, who decided that cooperation with an evil regime was incompatible with his Christian faith and he therefore refused to be conscripted. Advised to compromise by his priest and his bishop he rejected this path, was put on trial and was executed in Brandenburg prison on 9 August 1943.(See under Case Studies)

Some COs, especially Catholics, believed in the Just War theory but were opposed to the Nazi regime. Another Austrian, Father Franz Reinisch, like Jägerstätter, was one of these; he refused to take the oath because Nazi Germany was an aggressive state and he was beheaded in 1942. Christian pacifists included Franziskas Stratmann, a theologian who founded a Catholic peace movement which had a large following in the 1920s. Monsignor Dr Max Josef

Metzger, a priest who believed strongly in union of the Christian churches and who had founded an organisation for the regeneration of the Church, was imprisoned three times and finally beheaded on 17 April 1944; he had drawn up a plan for a new Germany after the Nazis but had entrusted it to a Swedish woman who turned out to be a Gestapo agent. Two men who were influenced by the evangelical pacifism of Metzger were Michael Lerpscher, a peasant, and Josef Ruf; although they were willing to serve in the medical corps this was refused and they were executed in 1940. Professor Johannes Ude of Austria was a priest who not only opposed war but also capital punishment and was an advocate of vegetarianism; he wrote many articles over 50 years and survived the war in spite of the attentions of the Gestapo.

Bernhard Lichtenberg, Provost of St Hedwig's Cathedral in Berlin had opposed Nazism from the beginning and when asked by the Gestapo commissioner how he felt towards Hitler replied: "I have only one Führer, Jesus Christ". He collected clothes and food ration cards for Jews and he prayed publicly every evening for them. He was sentenced to two years imprisonment in May 1942 and on expiry of the sentence was sent to Dachau but died on the way in November 1943. Another priest, Hermann Hoffmann, a professor at the University of Breslau, head of a convent, and a member of the pacifist Fellowship of Reconciliation (FoR), worked for reconciliation between Germany and Poland throughout the Weimar period and survived the Nazi period. Josef Scheuer took St Francis as his moral guide and refused to bear arms and was imprisoned in Sachsenhausen. Two brothers, Josef and Bernhard Fleischer, objected to modern warfare as they considered it to be indiscriminate mass killing but they escaped death sentences.

One solitary Baptist, Albert Herbst who was a mechanic, broke with his Church along with his wife when it allowed Nazis in uniform to take communion. He was executed in 1943 although the president of the military tribunal passed the sentence reluctantly.

He addressed him: "Herbst, you have made it extremely hard for us to come to a decision. We are all convinced you are indeed a sincere Christian. But alas there is no way out; there is no way we can get around the severity of the law". [Brock and Socknat p.374] Two clergy of the Confessional Church, Ernest Friedrich and Wilhelm Schumer agreed, for the sake of their families, to serve in the medical corps.

Dr Hermann Stöhr of Stettin, Secretary of the German FoR and a professor of Political Science, was prosecuted as a CO and executed on 21 June 1940 for "undermining the morale of the armed forces". Gerhard Halle was a friend of Stohr and like him also a First World War veteran but when recalled as a former reserve officer in 1942 refused to serve as he had become a Quaker. The army board surprisingly let him go free and did not inform the Gestapo which would no doubt have resulted in a different outcome. A woman FoR activist and outspoken anti-Nazi, Elizabeth von Thadden, founded a girls' school which continued to take Jewish girls but was eventually taken over by the state. She then worked for the Red Cross during the war but was arrested for belonging to a subversive discussion group run by Hanna Solf of the Confessional Church and was executed in 1944. Another man who had served in the German forces (as a naval officer) in the Great War was Heinz Kraschutzki who later joined the German Peace Society and edited its weekly paper. Since it sometimes published news about secret German rearmament he escaped to Spain before he was arrested but was imprisoned in Spain where he remained until 1945. He then returned to Berlin and remarried his wife who had been compelled to divorce her husband in order to keep her children.

The Austrian Jehovah's Witness Franz Zeiner declared that no genuine "follower of Christ could bear arms for whatever cause" and was executed in 1940, aged 31. [Brock and Socknat p.378] Another Austrian Pierre Ramus, a very active member of the War Resisters International and a Nazarene, hid in different houses in

Vienna before swimming across a river into Switzerland where he was imprisoned because he did not have a passport. On release he was taken across the border into France and left there. He was captured and spent some time in an internment camp, then managed to get to Spain and then to Morocco and eventually to a ship sailing from Casablanca to Mexico where he hoped to join his wife who had herself traveled from country to country. They were never reunited as he died on the seventh day at sea.

Gertrude Luckner was English born but her parents died when young and she was brought up by a German couple in Freiburg. She was a Quaker until her early thirties when she became a Roman Catholic. She joined the German Catholic Peace Movement and from 1938 worked for the aid organisation Caritas. She organised food parcels for German Jews deported to Poland and also travelled to German cities to take help to Jews and to organise the escape of some to Switzerland. On one of her train journeys in November 1943 she was arrested by the Gestapo and interned in Ravensbrook. She survived and continued social work after the war and promoting Christian-Jewish understanding.

Carl von Ossietzky, an editor and pacifist, exposed the secret rearming of the Weimar Republic in his newspaper and aroused opposition from the political right. In 1931 the author of the article, Walter Kreiser, and the editor were charged with treason and espionage. Found guilty they were given sentences of 18 months. But Kreiser left Germany leaving Ossietzky to serve his sentence. After Hitler became Chancellor in January 1933 Ossietzky was imprisoned again and spent the next few years in different concentration camps. However in 1935 he was awarded the Nobel Peace Prize and although pressured to decline it he accepted it although he was unable to attend the ceremony. It was a very contentious choice even within the Nobel committee and the Norwegian King did not attend the ceremony. Ossietzky was kept under Gestapo surveillance in hospital and on 4 May 1938 he died of tuberculosis.

In the Netherlands the pacifist society Kerk en Vrede (Church and Peace) was formed in 1924 as a largely Protestant body; at its peak in 1932 it had more than 9,000 members but was banned within a year of the German occupation. At first its journal continued to appear and it attacked the Nazi doctrine of Blood and Soil with its implication of anti-Semitism. One of its leading members, the theologian Gerrit Jan Heering, had written a widely read defence of Christian pacifism called *The Fall of Christianity* (1929). On 20 March 1941 Kerk en Vrede was dissolved and its property confiscated. However the executive committee continued to meet and some branches continued to operate. Thousands of circular letters were issued emphasising the Christian spirit of mercy rather than hatred. Church ministers preached against conforming with Nazi edicts especially regarding Jews.

One of its most active members was Rev J J Buskes. When the Dutch Nazi Anton Mussert announced in a speech that the military success of the German forces showed God's blessing this was attacked by Buskes in the journal of Church and Peace as an 'atrocious heresy'. Buskes also supported a call by Rev F Kleign to use the Nieuwe Kerk in Amsterdam as a place of refuge for Jews who were now being rounded up; although it was unlikely to save them it would at least be a witness. Buskes wrote several pamphlets one of which was a warning to school boards not to allow any political interference in the schools. He experienced three periods of imprisonment, the final one being after he had preached to a full church, condemning National Socialism in unambiguous terms.

The first Dutch Reformed minister to be arrested was N Padt, who was a member of the executive committee of Church and Peace; his second imprisonment lasted from October 1942 to May 1945, latterly in Dachau. At least 60 Reformed Church ministers helped Jews which led to their imprisonment. Rev J Cohen, a fiery preacher of Jewish descent and member of Church and Peace died in Dachau in 1942, probably gassed due to his Jewish descent. One who suffered for anti-militarist writing was the poet Jan Bosdriesz, a member of the Brotherhood in Christ (FoR) who ended up in Sachsenhausen and was liberated by the British only to die a few days later. Krijn Strijd, who spent a year in a concentration camp, protested in late 1944 against an Advent message from the Protestant churches which referred to the cruel actions perpetrated in the current war. He pointed out that such actions were to be expected during any war and the church protest should have been against war itself. After the war J J Buskes criticised the churches for not speaking out enough on war as a denial of Christianity.

A Dutch couple, Wilto Shortinghuis and his wife Marie, who were pacifists inspired by Gandhi and Albert Schweitzer, began by sheltering a Jewish doctor and his wife on their farm and then increased the number until there were twenty but felt guilty when they had to turn away others. Henk Huffener came from a Catholic family active in the Resistance but as a young man he was influenced by Betty Cadbury, a Quaker who married Dutchman Kees Boeke who himself ran a progressive boarding school. Henk came to believe that armed resistance was mainly counter-productive. He aided many Jews by finding homes for them and gathered money from wealthy Jews in hiding to help supply others with essentials. Eventually arrested he was sent as a slave labourer to Germany to work in a weapons factory where he sabotaged engineering parts. When released, in poor health, he returned to rescuing and after the war he settled in Britain as a protest against former collaborators who were holding high office in post-war Holland.

In Denmark the government remained in power until August 1943. The German occupation was mild in comparison to other occupied countries partly because the Germans wished to ensure regular supplies of agricultural products. Aldrig mere Krig (AmK) or No More War was founded in 1926 and became affiliated to the War Resisters' International founded in 1921. It was anti-militarist and pro-nonviolence. Unlike Kerk en Vrede in the Netherlands AmK was not a religious body. Helping COs was a large part of its work. It also pointed out that the Danish Army Manual, like other countries' army manuals, showed explicitly how young men are taught to kill other human beings. AmK also promoted the idea of collective nonviolent action. The general strike against the Kapp Putsch in Germany after the First World War, and the German resistance against the occupation of the Ruhr by the French in 1923 were discussed. The nonviolent Indian independence movement led by Gandhi was known of partly through Ellen Horup and Esther Faering Menon who worked with Gandhi in India.

When war began on 1 September 1939 the Danish government declared its neutrality and AmK supported this position. When Finland was attacked by Russia on 30 November, however, there was much popular Dutch support for the Finns which the AmK did not go along with. On 9 April 1940 Denmark was occupied with very little fighting. The AmK took the line that Danes should differentiate between the Nazi regime and the individual German soldiers. On 12 April the Government banned meetings except religious services. The AmK leadership recommended observance of Government orders, that is no demonstrations, political speeches or distribution of leaflets. On 12 September the ban on public meetings was lifted. AmK's journal continued to be published and it included criticism of Germany's treatment of Jews. In time Danish-German relations deteriorated and on 29 August 1943 the Government resigned, the armed forces were disbanded and the soldiers interned. As strikes and sabotage increased AmK members discussed the issue of sabotage. The famous Dutch pacifist Bart de Ligt had produced a *Plan of Campaign against All War and All Preparations for War* which included sabotage against bridges and railways. The AmK officially came out against sabotage since this might lead to violence against people. However some members did become involved in sabotage which caused controversy in the organisation at the end of the war. At the AmK's AGM in January 1946 it reaffirmed its nonviolent stance. The organisation lost few members during the war: in 1939 it had 1525 and in 1945 it had only fallen to 1404. The Danish and Norwegian branches of the WRI kept in touch and Danes sent Red Cross parcels to Norwegian prisoners in Germany.

There was little pacifist tradition in Norway but during the 1930s some pastors and theologians developed a pacifist belief. In April 1938 a group of Christians issued a statement that all war was a violation of the spirit of Christ; the group included some prominent Christians. Later that year a Norwegian Pastors' Pacifist Union formed; by March 1942 it had 87 members. However many who had pacifist sympathies had now begun to have doubts. First the Russian attack on Finland in 1939, followed by the invasion of Norway itself in April 1940 led to many abandoning their pacifist beliefs. But some stood firm. Andreas Seierstad, professor in the Lutheran School of Theology, maintained his pacifist conviction but cooperated with the civil resistance. Kristian Schjelderup, theologian, who was a pacifist from his youth was influenced by Albert Schweitzer and Gandhi. He strongly believed that good would conquer evil; he survived the occupation and became a bishop after the war.

The Jehovah's Witnesses as elsewhere were Conscientious Objectors and their numbers, a few hundred, actually grew during the war. There were only about 80 Quakers in Norway, the leading figure being Ole Olden, a school principal in Stavanger. He edited two journals which were banned by the Germans and he was taken as a hostage to Grini prison outside Oslo. A few other Quakers were imprisoned.

A branch of the War Resisters' International, FmK, had formed in Norway in 1937 on the initiative of Olaf Kullmann, who had been a captain in the Norwegian navy during WWI but became an ardent opponent of war. The other leading figure in the FmK was Dr Lilly Heber (who had written on Krishnamurti). In 1939 it had 235 members. Kullmann spoke around the country from spring 1940 to summer 1941 until arrested in June. He refused to give a guarantee that he would stop his peace lecturing and was therefore sent to Sachsenhausen camp in Germany where he died on 9 July 1942. Some other members of the FmK, which was banned, were arrested and some tortured but they remained firm. A leading FmK pacifist, Johanne Gjemoe, who was close to the Quakers in outlook stated after the war that nonviolent action requires preparation and training, comparable to military training, to be really effective. Diderich Lund, who participated in the nonviolent resistance until he had to flee abroad, believed that pacifists would have achieved more by open, uncompromising resistance. His wife Sigrid Lund helped Jewish children escape across the border into Sweden.

The Women's International League for Peace and Freedom was formed in 1915 and the Norwegian section (IKFF) in the same year. In June 1940 the national board of the IKFF sent a circular to its members to encourage them to work as they saw fit for the principles they believed in. The organisation was banned in August 1940 and its office seized but records had been removed beforehand. Many of the members joined the nonviolent resistance including its leader, Marie Lous Mohr, who was arrested in January 1943 and spent two and a half years in Grini prison. One of the most effective acts of resistance was initiated by Helga Stene against the Nazis' attempt to form a compulsory youth service. A letter of protest was sent by some 200,000 parents to the relevant department and the plan was abandoned.

In France most of the pacifist opposition came from Protestant members of the French section of the Fellowship of Reconciliation. There was one case that was outstanding and that was in the village of Le Chambon in the south of France where the pacifist pastor Andre Trocmé was the instigator. This is related later under case studies. Marc Sangnier was the principal Catholic opponent of war who influenced many young Catholics in this period. His main contribution during the occupation was making his printing facilities in Paris available to the nonviolent resistance. In October 1942 the journal *Résistance* first appeared and it was followed by about 2,000 different leaflets.

Jewish Resisters and Rescuers

In April 1933 the first of the Nazi Acts was enacted and the Jewish population began to look at potential legal protection. As a result of the post-war Geneva Convention of 1922 racial discrimination was outlawed in Upper Silesia. The case selected was Franz Bernheim, of Upper Silesia, who had been dismissed from his warehouse employment, in a petition to the Council of the League of Nations of 12 May 1933. A report on the position of the Jewish population of Upper Silesia was presented by the Irish delegate, Sean Lester. The Acts, he believed, infringed the right of equal treatment and should not be applied in the part of Silesia covered by the Convention of 1922. Judgement went against the Reich Government and the German delegate gave promise that Bernheim would be compensated and that the Geneva Convention would be honoured in Silesia. This was followed in September 1933 by a letter from the Association of Synagogues of Upper Silesia to the German Foreign Office claiming continuing discrimination and its intention of petitioning the League again. To avoid humiliation this time the Minister of the Interior met with Jewish representatives and the Geneva Convention was then enforced until 1937 when supervision expired. [Housden pp.121-2]

Germans Jews were highly assimilated but now they began to create or strengthen Jewish organisations. A leading figure in this was Rabbi Leo Baeck. In schooling, economic life, professional groups, cultural life, Jews were encouraged to co-operate more. Welfare organisations helped those in need and many Jews were prepared for emigration. Funds were raised from better off Jews and distributed to as many as one third of the Jewish population in 1935. The Reich Association of German Jews was established in September 1933 to co-ordinate these activities. In 1942 the leaders were sent to Theresienstadt.

A very different approach was initiated by a group of young German Jews who started meeting in 1933 and they became known as the Baum group after Herbert Baum their principal founder. They were mostly communists and they put up anti-Nazi posters in Berlin. After 1939 they worked in a Siemens factory in special Jewish departments. They were not believers in nonviolence and after they set fire to an anti-Soviet exhibition in 1942 Baum and others were arrested. Baum was tortured but did not identify any of his co-conspirators and was then executed. However 500 others were arrested and 250 of these were shot and the remainder deported. Only two of the group survived the war. [Housden pp.135-6]

Emigration was a route which many took although it entailed in many cases giving up most of their savings. Between 1933 and 1937 about 130,000 Jews left Germany (20% of the 1933 total) and a similar number left following Kristallnacht in 9-10 November 1938 so that by October 1941 only 164,000 Jews remained in Germany.

One technique of noncooperation was not to register with the authorities. In Berlin the mother of Valentine Senger put down "None" on a school form identifying his religion. This meant that the family had to stop going to the Jewish relief kitchen for food or associating with other Jews; they were fortunate not to look obviously Jewish.

Berthold Jacob emerged from the First World War a pacifist and as a journalist he exposed secret rearming during the Weimar republic. In 1932 he emigrated to Strasbourg where he led the exiled German League for Human Rights. On a visit to Switzerland in 1935 he was kidnapped by the Germans but he was released 6 months later through the intervention of the Swiss Government. He then went to Paris and then on to Lisbon but was kidnapped by the Germans again, imprisoned, and died in a Berlin hospital in 1944.

Kurt Hiller was a Jew whose pacifism stemmed primarily from his socialist beliefs. In 1926 he founded the Group of Revolutionary Pacifists and urged the League of Nations to abolish conscription in all countries. He was imprisoned in a concentration camp in 1933 and 1934 but then emigrated.

In Venice, Giuseppe Jona, Professor of Medicine and leader of the Jewish community there destroyed the records of Venetian Jewry and then killed himself to prevent the Nazis getting hold of the names.

A Zionist youth organisation in the Netherlands smuggled Jewish orphans to Switzerland and Spain.

The Jewish Scouts, Eclaireurs Israélites de France (EIF), founded in 1923 turned into a rescue organisation during the war. In 1939 they founded children's homes in SW France and after the occupation the EIF moved into the Vichy zone but continued to function illegally in Paris also. The EIF were dissolved in November 1941 but they were able to continue activities under Scoutisme Français providing Jewish children with identity papers and finding safe houses or helping them to escape until they were finally dissolved in January 1943. Their efforts saved a few thousand children.

One of the most flamboyant rescuers was Laszlo Szamosi, a Jewish property dealer who when the Nazis took over Hungary bought Christian identity papers for himself and his family. He went to a home for orphaned or separated Jewish children where his wife volunteered to teach and he provided food and other essentials. He and his wife found out from the children the names of the parents who might still be alive and made up Swiss passports which he took to the detention camps and got the 'owners' released. He met Raoul Wallenberg doing the same thing. Through a contact at the Spanish embassy he obtained passes issued by them for Jews and then gave them to Wallenberg to take to the frontier where they were given to Jews to prevent them being deported. When these Jews consequently got sent back to Budapest he helped them find safe houses. He even got himself taken on to the staff of the Spanish embassy. When the Spanish staff fled in December 1944 Szamosi continued on and worked with Italian Giorgio Perlasca who similarly moved into the Spanish embassy (see Wallenberg later). He then raised a Spanish flag at the children's home which protected them from the Hungarian fascists, the Arrow Cross. He dressed in Arrow Cross style with fur-trimmed coat and hat, and confidently strode through Arrow Cross lines. Near the end of December, Wallenberg, Szamosi and other neutral diplomats tried to prevent the 15 children's homes housing 5,000 children from being moved to the General Ghetto. The condition of the children was such that hundreds died during January to March 1945. Szamosi and his family survived the war and settled in Palestine.

In the Lodz ghetto in Poland demonstrations and strikes occurred over food shortages and wages in January 1941. It began with cabinet makers and then tailors and textile workers but Chaim Rumkowski, the leader of the Judenrät, the Jewish Council, would not give concessions even when children picketed his home and the protests collapsed after a week.

Suicide, and there were many, could be viewed as a form of resistance. Going into hiding was another. Praying as they were led to their deaths could be viewed as another. And so too Rabbi David Shapiro refusing offers of shelter from Warsaw Catholics in order to stay with his people.

But there were only a few occasions when Jews destined to be shot at the graveside resisted or tried to escape. Generally their spirit had been broken by the experiences leading up to their end.

Child Rescuers

Children often became involved in rescuing but it was usually through their parents' involvement. Very young children were not told the truth about those being hidden but rather were given a plausible explanation for the strangers' presence such as that they were distant relatives or that their home had been destroyed. Older children might help actively by being guides and couriers. Children didn't have the same awareness of the danger as the adults, and adolescents especially often did not grasp the danger they were exposed to. One difficulty they faced was the need to distance themselves from those of their friends who did not have to keep the secret they needed to.

Pania Wywiad in Warsaw became aware of the possibility of outbreak of war at the age of nine and shortly after that her father was called for military service. When German planes bombed the city her family rushed to the basement of their apartment. Her sister became hysterical at the sound of the siren and her brother developed a stutter (which became permanent) because of the frequent bombardment. Pania comforted them and went out for water, this action helping to overcome her fear. When the country was occupied by the Germans their father came home and then joined the underground while their mother began to take in Jews and others sought by the Nazis. A teacher she admired set up an underground classroom which Pania attended. Pania then began to deliver food and medicine and letters to underground members using the canal system under the streets of Warsaw. She started to watch the movements of the German soldiers and listened for any information that might be useful, but her main activity was escorting Jews out of the ghetto and finding hiding places for them. This included a family of mother, father and two daughters whom she successfully led to safety from the ghetto. In August 1944 the Warsaw Uprising began and Pania's father and brothers joined it. Gas, electricity and water were soon cut off and pro-German Ukrainians roamed the streets raping women. Pania and her mother were driven out of their home and forced onto a cattle truck destined for Auschwitz where on arrival they were put in separate blocks. Pania was in a block with girls of all ages. She was by now 14 and one day she fell ill and was put in a block for the sick. Here a Russian woman, who like all the prisoners was starving, came into the cellblock and slipped a precious piece of bread to her daughter and this act of love gave Pania hope. On 12 January 1945 she and her mother were were freed by the Russians and they returned to Warsaw where in time Pania became a special education teacher and worked at the Institute of Pediatrics with sick and chronically ill children.

In 1941 Stanislaw Wlodek, a Polish underground activist, was asked to hide a two-year-old Jewish boy. He and his wife agreed to take Jurek and they expected their nine-year-old and seven-year-old sons could help too. But a year later the Germans found a shortwave receiver in their house. Stanislaw managed to escape to the woods but his wife was arrested (and died in Auschwitz in 1943). The two boys, Janusz and Krystn, were left with the responsibility of looking after the younger boy. They lived on the food in the house until it ran out and then worked for local farmers for food, sometimes taking the Jewish boy with them and passing him as their nephew, but sometimes they left the boy for hours on his own. After some months a local woman began spreading the word that Jurek was a Jew but Stanislaw heard of this and quickly arranged for his sister who lived in a nearby village to take the boy who survived to liberation and was reunited with his mother. The two boys survived on their own.

Esther Warmerdam was eleven-years-old living in a large house outside Amsterdam with eleven sisters and brothers when her father started to invite people to stay with them. The reason he gave the children was that the strangers were hungry and more food was available in the countryside. One boy, Paul, was introduced to Esther as he was the same age. He had dark wavy hair and an aloof manner which Esther did not like; because he did not mix well with the children they called him Zandhaas after a sand rabbit that did not mix with other animals. One day he screamed "I'm not a rabbit! I'm a Jew! I'm a Jew!" The children did not understand but the father decided he needed to explain who these strangers were and why they needed to be there. From then on Esther decided she would keep her friends out of the house and she would help her father to protect these people. The Warmerdam's house was searched a number of times by the Germans. A plan was worked out for these terrifying occasions involving going out of the girls' bedroom window and along a roof to a flat part of the roof; the father organised games to prepare the children for these events. Between 1942 and 1945 more than 200 children were saved from deportation by the Warmerdams.

A rescuer's life was largely taken over by the effort of keeping safe those being hidden. In the case of Joop and Will Westerweel they sent their own children away to safety meaning that they sacrificed normal family life. More often the parents involved their children in the rescuing process thus putting a considerable burden on their children. If the rescuing was unsuccessful and those hidden were discovered either the rescuers were punished themselves, and this could mean death, or if they avoided being caught there remained the guilt of having failed and this could last a lifetime. After the war many child rescuers took up helping careers of various sorts. Helena Podgorska who helped care for thirteen Jews developed speech problems, which was a common effect of such experiences, and had nightmares for years but nevertheless she became a doctor in order to help others. Just as with adult rescuers their post-war lives were strongly influenced by the rescue experiences.

One of the more unusual rescues was not that of a Jew but of a young Christian woman by a Jewish boy. Nonna Lisowskaja, a well-to-do Russian from the Ukraine, got caught up in the chaos following the German occupation and in August 1942 she and her mother – the father had been beaten to death by German soldiers – were put on a freight train along with other women to be used as slave labourers in Germany. Near Lodz in Poland the train slowly came to a stop and they were given some water and a piece of bread. Various trains were being sent to different destinations from there and fifteen-year-old Nonna noticed a truck full of Jews and in particular an emaciated boy. When the Germans were busy she managed to slip out of her carriage and go over to the boy and gave him her bread. But before she could return to her truck the train with the Jews began to be unloaded and she got caught up in the mass of people who were driven to a field where she saw a few Jewish men digging a ditch. When the crowd reached the ditch they were made to spread out along the edge. The boy and his mother had kept close to Nonna and the boy now pulled her in front of him while the mother clung to the boy. Then the Germans began to shoot the Jews in the head and they toppled into the ditch. When the soldiers were close the boy gave Nonna a hard push so that she fell into the ditch and shortly afterwards the mother screamed "Nathan!" and they were both shot. Nathan's body fell on top of Nonna and she lay still, covered in mud and blood. When she opened her eyes after the killing had finished and the soldiers moved on she saw Nathan still clutching the piece of bread. With difficulty she dragged herself out of the ditch and managed to rejoin her mother and the other women.

Resisters and Rescuers:
Some Case Studies

THE WHITE ROSE GROUP MUNICH 1942-43 –
GENERAL POLITICAL OPPOSITION IN GERMANY

Hans, Sophie, Inge, and Werner Scholl were born in the quiet town of Kochertal but later moved to the city of Ulm on the Danube. Their father Robert had been mayor in several small towns in southwest Germany and when he settled in Ulm he opened an office as a tax and business consultant. He was a man of strong opinions and was outspoken too. He served as a medic in the First World War. During the War he met his future wife Magdalena who was a nurse.

The Nazis came to power when Hans was 15 and Sophie 12. Roaming the countryside in groups known as Wandervogel was a popular pastime of youths of that period and Hans was keen on this activity. Later, he and his brothers joined the Hitler Youth, before it became compulsory, although their liberal minded father was not at all happy about it. They enjoyed the outings and the company but when Hans was forbidden to sing foreign songs he was annoyed. In spite of this he was chosen as flag bearer of his troop for a rally at Nuremberg but he was disappointed at the strict conformity required. Then a book by Stefan Zweig that he was reading was taken from him because it was considered not fit to be read by the new Germans being created, Zweig being Jewish. Finally he was ordered to surrender a flag that had been specially made by his troup and this infuriated him so much that he struck the senior group leader. For Hans this was the end of the Hitler Youth. He realised his father's judgement was right.

The boys then joined a group called Jungenschaft which went on hikes and camping in all kinds of weather and they wrote up their experiences in elaborate magazines and an Excursion Book. They fenced, skied and read together, went to concerts and films and plays. They loved the art of Franz Marc, van Gogh, and Gauguin. In the summer of 1937 Hans and Inge visited two exhibitions of art in Munich. One was the House of German Art displaying Nazi approved art which the two visitors found unappealing while the exhibition of Goebbel's 'Degenerative Art' they found much more interesting. The Scholl children began a clandestine reading group around this time and circulated forbidden literature. But the Gestapo had decided to put an end to all illegal youth activity. Hans, doing his military service, was arrested and taken to Stuttgart; Inge and Werner were arrested at home and also taken to Stuttgart, while Sophie was taken too but released later that day. Inge and Werner were released after a week but Hans was kept for a month of interrogation. They and their parents were profoundly affected by the experience.

When the war started Hans, now studying medicine, was ordered to France to tend to the wounded. During this period he was reading Plato, Augustine, Pascal and the Bible. On reaching 21, Sophie had to do labour service and managed to get into kindergarten studies for six months. Unfortunately that was followed by six months of labouring on the land where the physical conditions were bad and she had in addition to endure ideological instruction.

Meanwhile their father had been arrested and detained for a time by the Gestapo after making a derogatory remark about Hitler to an employee, calling him a "scourge of humanity".

One day Magdalena Scholl was told by a Protestant nursing sister who worked in a home for mentally retarded children what had happened at the home – one day the SS arrived in trucks and began to remove the children by force. This was part of the 'euthanasia' programme to eliminate human beings whom the Nazis regarded as not fit to live. Protestant and Catholic bishops had already protested at the treatment of such individuals. The Catholic Bishop of Münster, Clemens Galen, for long a critic of the regime, in July 1941 made his strongest attack on the actions of the government from his pulpit – the Programme was "against God's commandments, against the law of nature, and against the system of jurisprudence in Germany". His sermons began to be distributed throughout the country and one day a copy arrived at the Scholl home when Hans happened to be at home. This gave him the impetus to act.

Hans became friendly with another medical student, Alexander Schmorell, son of a well-known Munich physician who had come from Russia. Through Alex, who had wide ranging interests as well as a great sense of humour, Hans met Christoph (Christel) Probst. He came from a well-to-do family who were also freethinking; the father was drawn to Indian religions in his later years. Christel married Herta Dohrn when he was 21 and by the time Hans met him the couple had two children. A fourth person, Willi Graf, joined the group – he was taciturn, a devout Catholic and the son of the head of a large business firm. From the beginning he was strongly anti-Nazi and had been arrested while at the University of Bonn. He served on the Eastern front as a medic and was haunted by the experience. All of the young men were studying medicine. Alex introduced Hans to Traute Lafrenz, also a medical student, and they developed a passionate relationship for a period.

Sophie moved to Munich to attend university also and there she met Hans' friends. The contrast between their lives devoted to healing and the slaughter of the war deeply troubled them and they began to think seriously of resistance to the regime. In June 1942 they started to write, duplicate and distribute leaflets. Many of these 'Leaflets of the White Rose' (the choice of the name is obscure) were posted to named individuals such as academics and civil servants but also to pub and restaurant owners. A second-hand duplicating machine had been bought and an artist friend had allowed the printing to be done in his basement.

The first leaflet includes the words:

"Who among us has any conception of the enormous shame that we and our children will feel when eventually the veil drops from our eyes and the most horrible of crimes – crimes that eclipse all atrocities throughout history – are exposed to the full light of day?" And later: "Adopt passive resistance – *resistance* – wherever you are, and block the functioning of this atheistic war machine before it is too late ..." [Dumbach & Newborn p.186, p.187]

Munich University like all universities in Nazi Germany at this time was firmly under the control of the Nazi Party. Lecturers had lost their posts and ended up in prison or concentration camps. In spite of this there were vestiges of the old liberal tradition. But to even hint at dissent from the official line was dangerous. Dr Kurt Huber taught philosophy there and Sophie Scholl attended his lectures which were open to students of other subjects and so Hans and other medical students attended also. Huber's interests were wide, including music (he had perfect pitch), but he was turned down for a professorship by the Nazi-run University. He was a political and social conservative but was vehemently anti-Nazi as he regarded them as revolutionaries. He had a severe limp and his hands and head sometimes shook. He was married with two children. Huber lectured mostly on the German idealists but had a particular interest in Leibnitz on whom he was writing a book. When lecturing he would occasionally throw out a dangerous remark which he could not resist such as when mentioning Spinoza – "Careful, he's a Jew! Don't let yourselves be contaminated". [Dumbach & Newborn p.87] One day in June 1942 Huber was invited to a reading evening in someone's home and decided to go. By chance Hans was also invited and at some point politics began to be discussed. There was general agreement that German culture was decaying but the view was also expressed that the only thing to do was to hang on and wait for this terrible period to end. At that point Hans angrily said: "Why don't we rent ourselves an island in the Aegean and offer courses on world-views?" This remark coming from a student must have annoyed many present but Huber's reaction was different and he said loudly: "Something must be done, and it must be done now!" [Dumbach & Newborn p.90] Hans and Huber agreed to meet again.

Sophie had only been at the university six weeks when she came across a 'Leaflet of the White Rose' attacking the regime and discovered it had been written by Hans. Shocked at first because of the danger it posed to all of the family she soon realised that it was the only way for her too. Three more leaflets followed which were distributed in other cities. One of the leaflets arrived in Kurt Huber's post a few days before he had another evening reading invitation this time to the home of Alexander Schmorell. Hans had called to ask him personally. The White Rose group were however disappointed as Huber said little at the meeting and left early.

During the summer Alex, Hans and Willi learned that they were to be sent to the Russian front along with others in their medical unit. The White Rose people had to dismantle the printing operation and before they went they held a party to which Huber was also invited. Huber still did not know the others were the White Rose.

It took more than a week for the train to reach the front and it stopped at Warsaw where they had a few hours. The state of the people there shocked them. When they reached Russia, Alex's ability to speak Russian meant that they could speak to peasants, as well as doctors, and this lifted their spirits, although it was forbidden to have such contact. It was November before they returned to Germany more determined than ever to do something.

Meanwhile Sophie returned home but was due to serve in a munitions factory for two months, something which depressed her. Worse still her father was sentenced to four months in prison for an anti-Hitler remark. Some evenings she took her flute to the prison wall and played the anti-tyranny song 'Die Gedanken Sind Frei' ('Your Thoughts are Free'). Most of her fellow workers were Russian women forced labourers living in miserable conditions.

By the time the White Rose group got together again the war was beginning to go badly for the Wehrmacht as they had been repulsed at Stalingrad and the winter was beginning. The subversives' plan now was to establish cells in other German cities. They knew by listening to foreign radio broadcasts that there were other resistance groups including a loose grouping called by the Gestapo the Red Orchestra, many members of whom had been arrested and executed. Hans and Alex believed they should link up with such opposition. They were able through a connection of Alex's to meet Falk Harnack, younger brother of the economist Arvid Harnack of the Red Orchestra who had been caught. They agreed on trying to build a united front ranging across the political spectrum. Traute Lafrenz went home to Hamburg and took leaflets with her to give to friends. This led to a branch of the White Rose being established there. Another was established in Berlin although the main contact there preferred to write his own leaflets as he disagreed with the anti-military tone of the originals.

In early December Hans and Alex visited Huber and told him that they were the White Rose which came as a surprise to him. They also told of the other opposition groups and when he heard that others were planning a putsch he decided to join the White Rose. As the movement spread Sophie was put in charge of the money; also when she paid visits to Ulm she printed leaflets secretly in the Martin Luther Church with help from friends and posted them out. The leaflets urged people to refuse to give to official collections of money, to boycott Nazi events, not to read Nazi newspapers, to sabotage industry and oppose the war. The leaflets were appearing in main cities such as Frankfurt, Stuttgart, Vienna, Freiburg, Saarbruchen, Mannheim, Karlsruhe, Salzburg, Linz.

A fifth leaflet was written by Hans and Alex with the title changed to 'Leaflets of the Resistance Movement in Germany'. Huber was critical of much of it but his objections were largely ignored. Many more of this leaflet were printed, perhaps 10,000, working during the night. In January 1943 Gestapo official Robert Mohr was assigned the task of uncovering the origins of these leaflets which were appearing in many cities in Germany. The distributors were taking the leaflets in suitcases by train to different cities and then posting them to other cities from there. For security they travelled singly and put the suitcase in one apartment and then found a seat in another.

On 13 January 1943 staff and students were expected to attend a meeting to commemorate the 470th anniversary of the founding of the University of Munich. No hall in the university was large enough for the gathering so the Deutsches Museum was used instead. Party and Government officials were also present. The White Rose students were not present as they had taken an oath not to attend such meetings but Kurt Huber was there. The audience was addressed by the Gauleiter of Bavaria, Paul Giesler, an anti-intellectual Nazi who after some praise for those who had served in the armed forces began to insult others who, he said, did not deserve to be there. He was particularly insulting to the women students who in his opinion should be in the home and giving birth to children. They should present the Fuhrer with a child every year! With a grin, he added, "And for those women students not pretty enough to catch a man, I'd be happy to lend them one of my adjutants." [Dumbach & Newborn p.132] This was too much and pandemonium ensued. Some women tried to leave but were arrested by SS men. Male students went to their aid and fights broke out. Female and male students who got out of the building started to march in the direction of the university. Special police forces had been called and the students dispersed but the demonstration soon became known about throughout the city. The White Rose people were euphoric and more determined than ever.

For loyal Germans devastating news was released to them on 3 February 1943 – the defeat of the Sixth Army of 300,000 men at Stalingrad. That night Hans, Alex and Willi painted slogans on walls around the city such as 'Freedom' and 'Down with Hitler'. Huber was affected as much as anyone by this terrible defeat and he resolved to write a leaflet. Around this time Falk Harnack arrived to meet the White Rose group. One important issue concerned the nature of post-war German society. Huber would not accept a role for the Communist Party. Huber's leaflet was discussed and it was acceptable to Hans and Alex except for one phrase – "support our glorious Wehrmacht". Huber insisted that it must remain but eventually he seems to have withdrawn his veto and the leaflet was printed although Huber was deeply disappointed and severed his link with the group.

On Thursday 18 February 1943 Hans and Sophie made their way to the university with leaflets in a suitcase. The lectures had not ended and they went up the stairs of the large inner courtyard and began to leave bundles of Kurt Huber's leaflet in the passages. Having some left they recklessly threw them down the stairwell. They were spotted by a member of staff who shouted: "You're under arrest". At that moment the students poured out of the lecture theatres and Sophie and Hans tried to leave the building along with the crowd but the custodian locked the doors and called the Gestapo. Robert Mohr and his men arrived but Mohr thought they were unlikely culprits until the leaflets were gathered together and put in the suitcase and were found to be a perfect fit. They were taken to Gestapo headquarters. Alexander Schmorell was outside the university and watched his two friends as they were taken away. He needed urgently to warn the others of the White Rose.

Robert Mohr decided to question Sophie and gave a colleague the task of interrogating Hans. Both Sophie and Hans remained calm under questioning. They denied everything at first but soon evidence from a search of their premises came up with evidence that the two were not the only ones involved. It was not long before Willi Graf and Christoph Probst were captured. Mohr tried to persuade Sophie that she had simply followed her brother and that Hitler had done great things for Germany. She responded: "You're wrong. I would do it all over again – because I am not wrong. *You* have the wrong world view." [Dumbach & Newborn p.151]

On Sunday morning Sophie, Hans and Christoph Probst were informed that they were accused of high treason. They were to be tried the next day by Roland Freisler of the People's Court, Berlin, a man noted for his ferocity. Sophie asked her lawyer calmly if she would be hanged or beheaded. He left the cell quickly.

On Friday the Scholl family in Ulm got the terrible news of the arrests but they could not get access to their children until Monday, if at all. Himmler wanted a quick trial and execution to forestall demonstrations. As Freisler raged against the accused Sophie shouted out: "Somebody had to make a start. What we said and wrote are what many people are thinking. They just don't dare to say it out loud!" Towards the end of the hearing the accused were given the opportunity of making a statement. Hans and Sophie declined but Christoph asked for clemency mainly because he had three young children and his wife was ill. As the sentence was about to be given Robert and Magdalena Scholl arrived and pushed their way into the court room. Robert wished to make a statement but the judge ordered his removal. As he was being removed Robert Scholl shouted out: "There is a higher justice! They will go down in history!" [Dumbach & Newborn p.158]

The sentence was announced and the three of them were led out. Werner Scholl who had come with his parents managed to touch Hans who said: "Stay strong. No compromises". They were taken to prison but remarkably the Scholl family were allowed in, against the rules, and briefly spoke to their son and daughter. Christoph Probst asked to be baptised a Catholic which was done. He was unable to see his wife and children. A small building housed the guillotine. Sophie was the first to be led there. As Hans was led there he turned towards the cells of the prison and shouted: "Long live freedom!"

In the following days and weeks many arrests were made, resulting in the trial of Alexander Schmorell, Willi Graf and Kurt Huber and eleven others of the White Rose group. The sentence for the three was the same – death. This time the executions were less hurried and their families were able to see them in prison. In the case of Willi Graf he was kept in prison for months while being interrogated about his contacts but was eventually beheaded like the others. The remainder received prison sentences except for Falk Harnack who was released as the Gestapo hoped he would lead them to others.

About the time of Willi Graf's execution members of the Hamburg Branch of the White Rose, who had been printing and distributing the Munich leaflets, were arrested. One of the group, Hans Leipelt, who was half Jewish, and studied at Munich had been given sanctuary in Professor Wieland's Chemistry Institute. After Kurt Huber's execution he had initiated collections for Clara Huber and the children. The Gestapo arrested him and after a year in prison he was beheaded at the beginning of 1945. Another six members of the Hamburg group were executed.

The rising of the students expected by the White Rose conspirators did not occur and a meeting organised by the students' union immediately after the execution of Han and Sophie drew a large number loyal to the regime. But knowledge of the White Rose groups spread throughout Germany and beyond and Kurt Huber's leaflet was reprinted and tens of thousands were dropped by Allied planes on German cities.

Scholl, Inge, *The White Rose: Munich 1942-1943*, Wesleyan University Press 1983

Dumback, Annette & Jud Newborn, *Sophie Scholl and the White Rose*, One World Publications Oxford 2006

ARISTIDES DE SOUSA MENDES (1885-1954) – PORTUGUESE RESCUER IN FRANCE

Aristides was a twin whose brother César in personality was serious and introverted in contrast to Aristides who had a generous and impulsive personality. The family were from the mountainous north of Portugal whose people are traditionally conservative and Catholic, in contrast to the south which is more radical, and they fitted into their family tradition. Liberalism was considered in their family to be unpatriotic because it was associated with Napoleon and his invasion of the country. The family was aristocratic and patriotic and their father was by profession a judge. The brothers entered Coimbra University, which was the only university in Portugal before 1911, and followed their father in taking up the study of law. They graduated in 1907 and both then entered the diplomatic corps.

In 1909 Aristides married his cousin Angelina who was to give birth to 14 children. In 1910 he was sent to British Guiana as Second Consul and it was that year that a republic was declared in Lisbon. In 1911 he was sent to Zanzibar; in 1917 to Brazil. In 1919 Aristides was suspended by the republican regime but reinstated the following year and sent to San Francisco. He was back in Brazil in 1924 and then to Spain in 1926.

There was a military coup that year led by General Carmona who assigned Antonio de Oliveira Salazar the finance ministry in 1928. Aristides de Sousa Mendes was then sent to Belgium as Consul General. In 1932 Salazar became Prime Minister and appointed César de Sousa Mendes as Foreign Minister although he was dismissed the following year. In 1934 there was a workers' uprising which was suppressed by Salazar. In 1936 a militia called the Portuguese Legion was created, and Government employees were forced to take an anti-Communist oath. In 1938 Aristides was appointed Consul General in Bordeaux. Portugal remained neutral throughout the Second World War but nevertheless the war was to have a great impact on Aristides.

A directive from the Foreign Ministry in November 1939 (Circular 14) said that no passports or visas were to be issued to those of undefined, contested or contentious nationality, stateless persons, Russians, holders of Nansen passports (available for those who had become stateless), or Jews expelled from their countries. In spite of this in February 1940 Sousa Mendes issued a visa to a professor from Barcelona who had been expelled and he was consequently reprimanded. Other cases followed. From 20 May refugees began to pour into Bordeaux. On 13-14 June Paris fell to the Germans and Bordeaux became the capital. The Portuguese consulate was now packed with refugees and Sousa Mendes wrote to Salazar for guidance – he was told to "enforce the regulations".

Sousa Mendes was facing a personal crisis. He gave shelter in his own home to Belgian Rabbi Chaim Kruger and his family but the application for a visa was turned down by the Ministry. Wrestling with his conscience he became ill and took to his bed. On the morning of the fourth day he had recovered. He said: "From now on I'm giving everyone visas. There will be no more nationalities, races or religions". With help from Rabbi Kruger, Sousa Mendes started issuing visas and enrolled the help of some of his many children too.

The Vichy Government was set up under Marshall Pétain and General de Gaulle flew to London. Sousa Mendes moved south to Bayonne on the Spanish border where he asserted his seniority at the consulate and continued to issue passports. The British Embassy complained about Sousa Mendes' actions and as a result Salazar ordered Sousa Mendes' actions to be stopped and he was stripped of his right to issue visas. The Spanish border was closed but Mendes managed to get some refugees through a minor crossing point. Among those saved were three members of the Rothschild family, the young Archduke Otto of Habsburg, the

Austrian writer Franz Werfel and his wife Alma (formerly married to Gustav Mahler), and the German writer Heinrich Mann.

On 30 June 1940 the Germans entered Bordeaux. Sousa Mendes issued a few more false passports and then returned to Portugal on 8 July. He went to Cabanes where many of the family resided and then he and his wife settled in Lisbon where there were many refugees. Salazar initiated an inquiry at which Sousa Mendes defended his actions but he was found guilty and demotion was recommended by the tribunal but Salazar went further and ordered his retirement (at 55). Sousa Mendes appealed partly because his financial position was desperate. In June 1941 the appeal was dismissed. The Jews in Lisbon were giving him a monthly allowance and allowed his family to eat at its soup kitchen.

When Hitler committed suicide on 30 April 1945 Salazar sent a telegram of condolence. Sousa Mendes had a stroke in May leaving his right arm paralysed. César, who was now Ambassador in Mexico, asked Salazar for his brother's rehabilitation but without success. Aristides and his sons signed a petition for free elections in Portugal; he also declared that Circular 14 was unconstitutional but they were ignored. César, now Ambassador in Switzerland, wrote to the foreign minister but there was no response. In the meantime Salazar was publicly proclaiming his country's 'hospitality' towards refugees, particularly Jews. How ironic when he had done his utmost to stop the issuing of passports to refugees.

In August 1948 Angelina died of a stroke in Lisbon and in April 1954 Aristides also died of a stroke. Sousa Mendes' children kept his memory alive and in February 1961 a tree was planted in the Garden of Righteousness in Jerusalem and in 1967 a commemorative medal was awarded by Yad Vashem (the memorial and research centre in Israel to the Shoah or Holocaust). After democracy returned to Portugal in 1976 his official standing was gradually restored and he was eventually posthumously created Ambassador by President Soares. In his memory a forest of 10,000 trees has been planted in the Negev representing the approximate number of Jews who were saved by his actions. Some have claimed that about 20,000, Jews and others, were saved by the actions of Sousa Mendes.

Fralon, Jose-Alain, *A Good Man in Evil Times* Translated by Peter Graham, Penguin 2001

THE PEOPLE OF ASSISI 1943-44 – RESCUERS OF JEWS IN ITALY

In July 1943 Mussolini was ousted and Italy signed an armistice with the Allies. The German army moved into Italy from the north and on 10 September Rome was occupied by the Wehrmacht. Italian Jews who had largely been left free of persecution were now threatened. Assisi was also occupied and the mayor Fortini, although a Fascist, resigned his post. The town had a population of around 5,000, of whom about 2,000 supported Mussolini, about 2,000 against, plus 1,000 monks, nuns and priests.

Giuseppe Nicolini Bishop of Assisi asked Fr Rufino Niccacci to help ten Jews he was sheltering in his palace to escape. Fr Rufino was of peasant family from the village of Deruta. In 1942, aged 31, he was appointed Father Guardian of San Damiano in Assisi and head of the seminary which he had attended as a student. Pretending to be pilgrims he took Jews by train to Florence where Cardinal Archbishop Costa helped. They were to go on to Genoa where there was a possibility of getting on board a neutral ship.

It was hoped that Assisi would be declared an open town but in fact the Germans occupied it. A further 30 Jews were now hidden in the convent of Poor Clares. With some difficulty the Abbess was persuaded by the Bishop to open the enclosed area for the Jews since monasteries were being searched. A Jewish scientist, Emilio Viterbi of the University of Padua, asked the mayor for help and the Sisters of San Colette sheltered the family.

A local printer called Brizi helped forge identity documents with invented names and addresses which were in keeping with southern Italians which was a good cover. About 160 Jews were now in Assisi but another 70 in Perugia needed documents too. On 23 November 1943 about 1,000 Jews were arrested in Florence and deported. Genoa was now closed to escapees. The Archbishop of Florence estimated that 40,000 Jews were in hiding in monasteries, churches and homes. 4,000 Roman Jews (half of the total) were hidden in 710 convents and 750 churches.

In Assisi, Lt Col Valentin Müller was in charge – a doctor and Catholic and a relatively humane soldier. Much more dangerous was the presence of SS Captain von den Velde. Giovani Cardelli was organising underground resistance in the town and had sheltered two anti-Fascist officers who had deserted. Canon Aldo Brunacci of San Rufino Cathedral established a school for the Jewish children and Christian instruction was given to those who were freely walking about the town in case they were questioned while Jews with accents and Jewish appearance were not allowed out of the monastery.

Cardinal Costa requested Fr Rufino to take a group of Jews across the Sangro river to Abruzzi. Pretending that they were pilgrims Fr Rufino asked the Colonel for a truck for the journey which they were given. However at the last stage of the journey the smugglers wanted more money so a mass was held in the local church and the collection used. The smugglers took the Jews through a forest and across a river and at the destination on the British side, oil, sugar and salt were obtained to bring back for the refugees in hiding. However on returning to Assisi Captain von den Velde informed Fr Rufino that no trucks would be available in future. Fr Rufino went to see Colonel Müller who told him that he had written to Field Marshal Kesserling asking for Assisi to be made an open city. There were now about 2,000 Catholic refugees from the south in Assisi.

The town was now made a hospital town for wounded German soldiers and 2,000 wounded were brought in so that the population of the town had almost doubled when the soldiers and refugees were counted. All the churches and monasteries were filled with Jews while the Catholic refugees were with local families. The basilicas of St Francis and St Clare were not used to hide Jews to avoid the risk of destruction of the buildings in the event of discovery. When one of the Jews, Clara Weiss, died she had to be given a Christian funeral.

A serious blow came when a group of young men travelling with documents for the Jews in Perugia were caught. The other centres were quickly informed but the men had been taken by the OVRA (Italian secret police). In Assisi, Captain von den Velde came to search the convent of San Quirico but the Jews there escaped in time through a tunnel which led to a forest. Professor Fano met them and said that San Colette had also been searched but the occupants had fled in time.

On 15 May 1944 Canon Don Brunacci was taken to Perugia for interrogation as a result of a Jewish boy sheltered by the Bishop having been discovered. However at the request of the Vatican the chief of police was persuaded to release the Canon, perhaps influenced by the fall of Monte Cassino to the Allies on 18 May.

The Germans now planned to blow up the buildings of Assisi but then an order came from Kesserling to make Assisi an open city – in fact the order was a forgery but it was effective. The SS captain then left Assisi for good. On 4 June Rome was taken by the Allies. The German wounded were evacuated from Assisi but before leaving, Müller went to see the Bishop and told him he was leaving all the medical equipment behind for their use. Müller then went to the church to pray and then met the monks, both Christian and Jew!

British tanks reached the outskirts of Assisi the next day. A ten-year-old partisan showed a way of cutting off the SS under the command of von den Velde and this was achieved with a battle. The refugees and others streamed out of the buildings to welcome the soldiers. Unfortunately the British confiscated the medical equipment so the inhabitants did not benefit as Müller had intended.

In 1950 Müller returned to Assisi with his wife and son and daughter, who were both medical students, and were given an official reception and attended mass conducted by Padre Niccacci. There was a hint that Müller had suspected that Jews had been sheltered in the town. Müller died the following year at age 60.

Fogelman, Eva, *Conscience and Courage,* Anchor Books 1994

Ramati, Alexander, *The Assisi Underground* as told by Padre Rufino Niccacci, Unwin Paperbacks 1985

AID WORKERS AND RESCUERS IN VICHY FRANCE

More than 20 internment camps were established in France, the majority of them in the unoccupied south of the country. In these were kept not only Jews but Communists, Gypsies, Freemasons and others considered undesirable. One of the worst camps was in the village of Gurs in the south-west close to the Pyrenees. Camp de Gurs had been established for Spanish refugees from the Civil War but from October 1940 Jews began to be settled there. The living conditions were terrible, the camp being covered in snow in winter and was very muddy in warmer weather, while the huts were poorly built and the water supply and food were inadequate. The women and children were separated from the men and boys of 14 upwards. On the other hand security was lax and thus various aid organisations were able to get in to help.

CIMADE was an aid organisation of mainly Protestant women. In 1940 Madeleine Barot became the General Secretary based in Paris who when she heard of the conditions in Gurs travelled there and managed to get admitted to the camp. She discovered that a new born baby had died and the officer in charge told her of the lack of nurses and clothes in the camp. She immediately said she would supply them although there were 16,000 people in the camp. Barot settled in a nearby village and found a nurse willing to help the many people there who were ill due to the conditions. They found a hut they could use and gradually nurses and social workers were recruited. Soon another organisation called Organisation de Secours aux Enfants (OSE) arrived. It had been founded before the Great War to work with destitute Jews in Russia but moved its headquarters to Paris in 1932. As Jewish families from Germany and Austria fled west, OSE set up children's homes in Montpellier and Lyons. A leading figure in the OSE was another Madeleine whose married name was Dreyfus. Due to the obvious need, in November 1940 twenty-five welfare organisations met in Toulouse to cooperate and this included Americans as the USA had not yet entered the war. The American Jewish Joint Distribution Committee, known as the 'Joint', was already involved in fund raising among Jews in America and they now channeled money to the camps. Quakers were also active and the World Council of Churches in Geneva got involved. Soon food and other essential goods were arriving with a particular focus on the children – footballs, books and even a piano were supplied too. Still there was insufficient food and the huts were not wind and rain proof and many died during the winter. In Gurs more than a thousand people died in 1941.

As there seemed to be no hope of Vichy authorities releasing the adults the aid organisations concentrated on the children. The OSE took the lead. They were already looking after 752 Jewish children whose parents had been deported in homes and other places around the country. Andrée Salomon of the OSE went round the different départements of the unoccupied zone trying to persuade the prefects to allow children from the camps to be settled in homes, schools or convents while other young women followed Andrée on bicycles searching for places to settle the children.

Another camp was Rivesaltes in the south-east on the Mediterranean coast. The huts here were of solid build but by the end of 1941 there were 20,000 inmates and conditions were no better than at Gurs. Starvation diet and insanitary living conditions created misery and disease. Permission was given to move the smallest children to a nursery in a deserted chateau and mothers pled with the aid workers to take their children. Small groups of children had been able to get on board ship for the USA leaving from Marseilles through the influence of Eleanor Roosevelt who obtained visas for children who had relatives in the USA; however they needed to be able to afford the escalating travel costs.

The USA and Canada were willing to take in 1,000 children each from southern France and Alice Resch, a Norwegian nurse with Quaker connections, had to choose 500 with help from a journalist Dr Ratner and a physician Dr Worms, both Jewish. However when the US Secretary of State criticised Prime Minister Laval the quota was reduced to 250. 150 children did depart for the USA in autumn 1941 and spring 1942 but when the Germans took control of the whole of France the remaining children were sent back to the camps.

By summer 1942 most foreign Jews had been deported from the occupied zone and on 4 July the Vichy regime accepted that their turn had come and agreed to deport 10,000 non-French Jews from the southern zone. The internment camps were now sealed off but some internees had permission to be outside the camps and they were now warned to hide in the countryside. Even those about to board ship had their permissions cancelled. Panic spread in the camps and some people committed suicide, or attempted suicide, rather than be deported. It was unclear whether children were to be included and so the rescuers urged parents to leave the children behind and they would look after them. The first train from Rivesaltes had 900 people on board including 82 children. Only 20 children had been rescued. The trains were bound for Drancy near Paris which was a gathering point for those to be sent on to the extermination camps in Poland. Conditions were once more atrocious. Between 17 and 31 August seven trains left for Auschwitz with 3,500 children on board.

Amidst all this darkness there was a chink of light. It came from a small camp on the outer fringe of Lyon called Vénissieux. It was a former military barracks. Lyon had a large population of resident Jews now increased by many more who had fled from the occupied zone. Early in the morning of 26 August 1942 police in threes started to round up Jews in Lyon, however the result fell far short of the quota as only 1016 Jews were picked up due to some police being less than thorough and warnings being spread too.

Two catholic priests now became involved. Père Chaillet and Abbé Glasberg (a Catholic convert with Jewish parents) had been working with refugees since 1941 and had founded L'Amitié Chrétienne which consisted of Catholics, Protestants and Jews. Cardinal Gerlier of Lyon was the chairman in spite of initially supporting Pétain. In the camp there was little order as instructions kept being changed. A number of rescuers including Andrée Salomon and Madeleine Dreyfus from the OSE and Madeleine Barot from Cimade got into the camp and started gathering evidence to support exemptions from deportation. Dr Jean Adam, a young doctor assigned by the authorities, cooperated with the team and recorded patients as suffering from severe illnesses so that they avoided deportation. But fear of what lay before them drove many to attempt suicide – 26 in one night alone.

By chance Abbé Glasberg intercepted a telegram from the Prefect to the Chief of Police informing him that children were not to be exempted from deportation. He acted immediately and in the dark he and other helpers went from family to family asking them to give over their children to L'Amitié Chrétienne while obtaining signatures of permission. They gathered 89 children. 545 Jews were put on the train that morning and only one survived. The 89 were taken to an abandoned convent and handed over to Madeleine Dreyfus and the OSE. When the Prefect discovered that not all children had been deported he ordered them to be found but word got to Dreyfus and the children were quickly scattered to safe places around Lyons.

As a punishment Père Chaillet was sent to a psychiatric hospital for two months while Glasberg went underground, changing his name and becoming a parish priest but continuing resistance by distributing anti-German leaflets.

From October 1940 Jews were legally discriminated against yet until 1942 there was no official opposition from church bodies. The Catholic Church in particular was very pro-Vichy as they saw Pétain as protecting traditional moral values. The population at large was relatively indifferent to discrimination against foreign Jews, however when they became aware of the brutal treatment of the foreign Jews by the Nazis and then learned that French Jews were going to be treated in the same way, attitudes changed.

Marc Boegner, President of the Protestant Reformed Church, typified the change that came over the clergy. Although naturally respectful of the state's institutions he wrote in March 1941 to the Chief Rabbi, Isaie Schwartz, to express solidarity with the Jewish people. At the same time he wrote to Admiral Darlan, Vice President of the Council at Vichy, to say that France must show respect for the individual. He mentioned in particular the 'disgrace' of the internment camps. In early July 1942 Boegner visited Prime Minister Laval to remind him that the Germans had not yet demanded the deportation of children under 16. Laval replied that children were needed to make up the quotas. As a result of the meeting Boegner asked Madeleine Barot and other Cimade workers to go immediately to Lyons to see what could be done to save the children.

The French Catholics at the Assembly of Cardinals and Archbishops in July 1941 had declared that France should display "sincere and total loyalty towards the established power". [Moorehead p.81] But this was not the position of some priests. The Jesuit Père Chaillet wrote a pamphlet which had a print run of 5,000 and was distributed in Lyons in late 1941. In it he said that the Christian had to be in the vanguard of opposition to racism. Further essays defending human rights followed during 1942 and another topic written about was rediscovering the Jewish roots of Christianity. Now some of the Catholic hierarchy began to speak out including the Archbishop of Toulouse, Mgr Jules-Géraud Saliège, who was partially paralysed. He dictated a pastoral letter to be read out the following Sunday. The Prefect heard of the intention and tried to stop it but most priests carried out the will of their archbishop and those who did not were rebuked and instructed to read it out the following Sunday. In the space of a few weeks 35 bishops and archbishops had spoken publicly and their messages in defence of the Jews were printed and distributed. However none of the bishops in the occupied zone spoke out.

In September 1942, 4,000 Protestants gathered at a farm for their annual gathering at which the situation of the Jews was a prominent topic. Afterwards Boegner went to see Laval again to strongly protest at the government actions without however expecting any change. He then went to Switzerland to ask them to allow refugees sent by charities to be admitted and received some satisfaction.

At Christmas 1942, 50 tons of clothing came from the American Friends Service Committee and toys came from Switzerland through Secours Suisse to be distributed in the camps.

An Alsatian doctor, Joseph Weill, a Jew descended from many illustrious rabbis, had gathered a team of doctors to operate through OSE helping in the internment camps. However he believed it was necessary for him to go underground and now made contact with an electrical engineer, Georges Garel, who had helped at Vénissieux. They met in a Lyon hotel and decided that the best way to save the children was to disperse them. Garel took on the identity of a travelling pottery salesman, hiding money and documents in his sample bag. He went to see Saliège, Archbishop of Toulouse, who gave him a letter of introduction to his most reliable priests. Money was to be supplied by the Joint. Jewish students who had not been deported would help as would young female social workers. The organisation became known as the Circuit Garel which operated through small cells. Andrée Salomon was in charge of recruitment and planning. She was officially in charge of the children's homes which were full of Jewish children which was surprisingly still allowed, but she also searched for places to hide other Jewish children. One of the convents often used for hiding was La Motte which was headed by a sophisticated, and formerly married, Mother Superior, Dolores Salazar.

Cimade was also turning to clandestine work and Madeleine Barot was in touch with Abbé Glasberg about safe houses. The Jewish Scouts, Eclaireurs Israélites de France, who had helped in Vénissieux were good at rescuing adolescents. Another priest, Abbé Gros, moved illegally across the Swiss border bringing back special treats hidden in his robes as well as showing the route for escapees until being suspected by the Gestapo he one day crossed the border and decided it was time to stay in Switzerland. The isolated villages of the Vivarais-Lignon plateau also began to be used for settling the children. Strangely, Jewish authorities still refused to acknowledge the danger Jews were in and recommended being open about their identity. In fact by September 1942, 38,000 Jews had been deported to Auschwitz and most had been gassed. The BBC broadcasts from London from July were saying that Jews were being massacred. But with opposition to the deportations by French people growing, Laval was having trouble meeting the German demands which was for 50,000 more Jews.

The last deportation was on 30 July 1944. On 15 August the Allies landed in the Côte D'Azur and on 19 August Toulouse was liberated. Many of Le Maquis joined the French army and went north to fight. After skirmishes between Germans and French everyone gathered in front of the city hall. Some reprisals occurred with abuse of collaborators and women who had been friendly with German soldiers. However those responsible for the abuse were later punished.

By the time France was liberated there had been about 75 deportations from France and about 80,000 Jews had been murdered out of 270,000.

Moorehead, Caroline, *Village of Secrets: Defying the Nazis in Vichy France,* Chatto & Windus 2014

Synnestvedt, Alice Resch, *Over the Highest Mountains,* International Productions 2005

RAOUL WALLENBERG AND OTHER DIPLOMATIC RESCUERS OF HUNGARIAN JEWS

Raoul Wallenberg was born in 1912 to a well-known and respected Swedish family whose father died of cancer before he was born. His mother Maj was the daughter of the first professor of neurology in Sweden. Her husband's father, Gustav, was Ambassador to Japan at the time. Maj remarried 6 years later and had 2 further children.

Raoul went to the USA to study architecture at which he was very successful. He in addition already spoke four languages. However his grandfather Gustav who took a great interest in him insisted that he study commerce and banking so Raoul went to South Africa for 6 months where he proved an excellent salesman. In 1936 his grandfather was Ambassador to Turkey where he met a

Jewish banker who offered Raoul an unpaid job in Haifa and there he met young Jews who had fled Europe. Raoul himself had a great great grandfather on his mother's side who was Jewish. In 1937 Gustav died and Raoul went into business with a German-Jewish refugee but the business did not flourish. Nor was his American architectural qualification recognised in Sweden and so in 1941 he joined a speciality foodstuff firm run by a Hungarian Jewish refugee, Koloman Lauer. Raoul could travel on the continent unlike Lauer and he visited Germany and then German-occupied France and Hungary on business. However he was dissatisfied with his life.

In the winter of 1942 he saw at the British Embassy in Stockholm the film *Pimpernel Smith* in which Leslie Howard (who in spite of his name was a Hungarian Jew) rescued Nazi victims. Raoul strongly identified with Howard as Pimpernel Smith.

Early in 1944 the War Refugee Board was set up by Roosevelt to aid those persecuted by the Nazis. In neutral Sweden the WRB got a committee together headed by Iver Olsen and they advised that someone go as a diplomat to Budapest with a large sum of money and empowered to issue Swedish passports to Jews so that they could escape to Sweden. Swedish Jews, however, did not welcome the prospect of a large influx of refugees in case of a negative impact on them.

The first choice of the committee was Count Folke Bernadotte, President of the Swedish Red Cross but he was refused permission by the Hungarian Government. Then Wallenberg's business partner Lauer put forward Wallenberg's name and he was accepted, in spite of his age, after he made a strong impression at interviews. His language skills and contacts on the continent would be useful. Wallenberg negotiated with the Foreign Office to be given an unusually free hand in the work. The Prime Minister had to be consulted and he gave his approval. Wallenberg would operate from the Swedish legation in Budapest. He was given a salary for two months and bribery was approved as a method for rescuing.

The greatest amount of money used by Wallenberg came from 'The Joint' with an account in Switzerland.

The situation in Hungary in 1944 was one of different power groups struggling for control. Within Hungary the Government changed a few times, the Germans reacted to these changes and there were different views on how to handle the situations that arose, and there were different groups trying to rescue the Hungarian Jews.

When Adolf Eichmann had first arrived in Budapest on 21 March 1944 two days after the German take over of Hungary he had tried to calm the Jewish leaders to prevent panic and a possible uprising such as in Warsaw. He said he needed labourers and would protect Jews. But within days they were forbidden to leave their homes and they had to give up telephones, radios and cars. They were expelled from the civil service and professions, and businesses had to be surrendered. He ordered Jewish Councils to be set up around the country. In the provinces Jews were put into camps and ghettos by the Hungarian gendarmerie (not the army or city police). Between 15 May and 10 June 1944 335,000 Jews in the provinces were deported. The deportations to Poland were so swift that the gas chambers could not cope and the number of trains had to be reduced. Hitler actually gave priority to trains for this deportation rather than for the retreating army.

In July Wallenberg went to Budapest via Berlin arriving in Budapest on 9 July at a time when the majority of the Budapest Jews were still resident there. The Hungarian Regent Miklos Horthy, who had received many appeals from international figures such as the Pope, President Roosevelt and the International Red Cross and who was also aware of the Red Army approaching, decided in self-interest to stop further deportations. Eichmann did not have enough manpower for the roundup and so appealed to Berlin. But Himmler accepted the suspension because he was trying to negotiate a peace with the Western Allies before the Russians arrived.

Wallenberg arrived when the tide had turned against Germany, and the Hungarians were worried about post-war retribution; nevertheless the Jews were still in great danger. Wallenberg redesigned the Swedish passport to make it look more impressive. The Hungarian Foreign Ministry gave permission for 1,500 passports but eventually it was raised to 4,500. Space was rented in houses for Jews who came under Swedish protection. The Swiss consulate had been successfully issuing a simpler document since 1942. A staff of 250 mainly Jews was built up by Wallenberg and they worked in shifts round the clock in a villa next to the Swedish legation. The Spanish minister at the legation in Budapest, Angel Sanz-Briz, issued letters of protection which he hoped the Hungarians would recognise because they wanted to maintain good relations with Madrid. Latin American missions followed. The Papal Nuncio Angelo Rotta issued baptismal certificates and safe-conduct passes to Jews (at the instigation of Archbishop Roncalli, later Pope John XXIII). In addition Wallenberg set up hospitals, nurseries and soup kitchens. The International Red Cross followed suit. Wallenberg's staff increased to 400 and they took only four hours sleep per night. Wallenberg observed that most of the Jews in Budapest were apathetic and not inclined to help themselves in spite of knowing about the extermination programme. Fellow Swedish diplomat Per Anger agreed. The Swiss diplomat Carl Lutz obtained an office block into which in time 3,000 Jews were crammed.

An Italian, Giorgio Perlasca, after witnessing the murder of a Jewish boy became a volunteer member of the Spanish legation. He looked for houses to place holders of the letters of protection issued by Sanz-Briz and placed 5,200 Jews. The Spanish flag flew over each building. But Sanz-Briz was forced to leave the country and the police prepared to enter the protected houses. Perlasca then pretended to be the legal representative of Spain and told the officials that Sanz-Briz had gone to a conference in Switzerland, and this gave the Jews continuing protection. When the Russians took Budapest, Perlasca was captured and put to work cleaning streets of rubbish and corpses and was later deported to Istanbul. Later he was able to return to Italy but he did not talk of his wartime exploits. In the late 1980s survivors remembering him placed notices in newspapers and in 1989 he was honoured at Yad Vashem.

On 14 July Eichmann sent an SS detachment to Kisteresa camp where they overpowered the Hungarians guarding 1500 Jews and loaded them onto a train. Dr Peto of the Jewish Council heard of this and phoned the son of Admiral Horthy who ordered the deportation to be stopped. Eichmann was furious and succeeded in taking the camp and deporting the Jews. He then got permission to increase the SS troops in Budapest to 9,500 and on arrival they paraded through the city. The leaders of the Jewish Council were arrested and brutally interrogated but Horthy forced Eichmann to release them after 24 hours.

In August Wallenberg drew up a new document, 'a protective passport' or Schutzpass, and had it printed by a Jewish-owned firm. It lacked support in international law but he negotiated with the Hungarian Interior Ministry who agreed to recognise it. This led to the release of some people from concentration camps.

Deportations were due to resume on 25 August which led to protests from the Swiss, Spanish and Portuguese diplomats and the Papal Nuncio Angelo Rotta. But then the Romanian Government of Antonescu collapsed and the country entered the war on the Allied side. It therefore became important that Hungary remain on Germany's side so Himmler halted the deportations and Eichmann was recalled for a period. The plan for Jews was to have them in camps in the provinces but the International Red Cross objected and declared none of them fit so the Hungarian government dropped the plan. Wallenberg was now running down his operation.

Over the summer, negotiations were conducted between a Jewish leader, Rudolf Kasztner, and the SS about exchanging a million Jewish lives for 10,000 trucks to be supplied by the British and Americans. Himmler was interested in pursuing this but no agreement was reached. However 1,700 wealthy Jews, including members of Kasztner's family, were released to Switzerland in exchange for gold and jewels. Kasztner was later murdered in Tel Aviv by Jews who thought he had betrayed them by negotiating with Nazis.

As part of an agreement between Eichmann and Kasztner, 15,000 Jews at $100 a head were sent for labour service around Vienna rather than to Auschwitz. However they had only light clothes to wear. Wallenberg went to the camp to negotiate with the commandant and managed to get 80 men released that day. The Red Cross supplied some clothes. As the general situation was unstable Wallenberg decided to stay on in Hungary.

As the Soviet Army drew closer Horthy tried to sue for peace with the Russians and on 15 October he announced over the radio that the war was over for them. Foolishly the Government did not secure the capital and the right-wing Arrow Cross Party took control and the Germans started to return. The SS kidnapped Horthy's son who had been planning to meet with Yugoslav partisans so Horthy surrendered and was sent into exile in Bavaria. The Arrow Cross occupied the radio station and announced that Ferenc Szalasi was now Leader of the Nation. Eichmann returned two days later. Most members of the Swedish legation left by train for home passing through Germany. Wallenberg continued his rescue efforts by managing to get Swedish-protected Jews released from a synagogue where they had been locked in by soldiers.

The new Interior Minister, Gabor Vajna, announced that Jews carrying foreign passports could not be protected. Wallenburg however had a useful personal contact in the new regime, namely the wife of the Foreign Minister Baron Gabor Kemeny. Wallenberg visited their home often and persuaded Kemeny to ask Szalasi to allow validation of neutral passports using the argument that this was one means of getting rid of Jews. Wallenberg also asked Baroness Erzsebet Kemeny, who was opposed to the Party's anti-semitism, to persuade her husband to broadcast this decision and he reluctantly agreed probably hoping to avoid prosecution at the end of the war. But this did not in fact save him and he was executed.

In the weeks before the coup the Arrow Cross Party had been expanded partly by taking in undisciplined youths from slum areas. They initiated a terror throughout the city and targetted Jews in particular. Wallenberg rode through the city on his bike trying to be everywhere and giving encouragement. Arrow Cross thugs were sometimes stopped by Wallenberg's passes which looked impressive.

In early November Eichmann started rounding up male Jews for labour service. They were kept in terrible conditions in a brickworks. Wallenberg and others from the Red Cross and Swiss legation went every morning to rescue those who had protective papers. The remainder were made to walk 240 kilometres to the Austrian border in snow without proper clothes. It took 7-8 days and they became known as the Death Marches. Wallenberg managed to give passports to some and put them on trains back to Budapest; assisted by Per Anger and others they travelled along the route taking food, medicine and clothing. Men from the labour battalions were also marched to the frontier and were put on board barges on the Danube where many committed suicide by jumping overboard. Even SS officers protested and Himmler summoned Eichmann to Berlin and ordered him to stop the marches. 15,000 Jews with Swedish and other protective passes were returned. However on 21 November a new march was started on Eichmann's orders. Wallenberg, Per Anger and some Jewish employees along with three large lorries carrying food and medicines and a doctor and nurses set off for the border town. On arrival names were taken to be added to Wallenberg's list. He carried a portable typewriter and forms to be completed and by this means rescued a few hundred people.

As the Allies bombarded the city, non-Jews left in columns. The Jews were herded into the two ghettos – the International Ghetto consisting of Swedish, Swiss, and Red Cross protected houses, and unprotected Jews in the General Ghetto. The normal population of the area of the International Ghetto was only 4,000 but eventually went up to about 40,000 so it was appallingly overcrowded. Passports were issued freely in large numbers and the totals concealed. Because of the cramped conditions disease spread readily so a hospital was set up using 6 apartments with 50 beds and ten specialist doctors. It opened on 2 December and later a fever hospital was established. They were well equipped thanks to Wallenberg's access to funds. Jews who did not have documents had to move to the General Ghetto where there were eventually about 70,000 people. In both ghetto areas the non-Jews displaced were furious. A wooden wall was built around the General Ghetto with Jewish money and Jewish labour. It had four entrances but no exits as it was a closed ghetto. There was a desperate shortage of food which Wallenberg used all his ingenuity to solve and this included the help of a Jewish canning factory owner who supplied the German Army.

After the October coup Wallenberg moved his main office to the Pest side of the city, closer to the Soviet Army and also the side where the ghettos were located. The office began with about 100 employees but grew to 340, which with their families was around 700. The two entrances were guarded by police. Branch offices were established elsewhere and the administration was meticulous in spite of the difficult circumstances. One section dealt with assaults on protected Jews and it worked round the clock. Wallenberg reported attacks to the police. Staff went out on rescue missions dressed in SS or Arrow Cross uniforms. One staff member, Ivan Szekely, spoke perfect German and had a authoritative manner that nearly always resulted in detained Jews being released. In spite of all efforts the Arrow Cross managed to kill about 50 Jews per day. One notorious murderer was a priest, Andras Kun, who is estimated to have killed 500 Jews – in the name of Christ; and a young woman Mrs Vilmos Salzer who was particularly sadistic. One method of killing was drowning in the Danube. Sometimes victims were just shot and their bodies thrown into the river but another was tying three people together and shooting the one in the middle so that when thrown in the river the one would drag the other two down. Wallenberg and others often went to the river at night to try and save people and on at least one occasion one staff woman and three men went to the river in mid winter and dived in, managing to pull out people who were then treated by doctors and nurses.

Sometime in December Wallenberg invited Eichmann to dinner to find out more about him. At some point during the evening he started to attack Nazi ideology and asserted that the Nazis were finished. Eichmann retaliated by saying his guest's diplomatic status would not protect him. Shortly afterwards Wallenberg's car was rammed by a large truck and Wallenberg went straight to Eichmann to protest.

On 22 December the Swedish Red Cross children's home was stormed and the staff taken away. A house in the International Ghetto was raided and 41 people taken to the Hungarian Gestapo HQ. Representatives of neutral countries drew up a protest note which Wallenberg took to the Gestapo HQ where it was denied that children had been taken. Wallenberg and Anger then went to the Deputy Foreign Minister. Three days later violation of children's homes was forbidden. Wallenberg's constant activity exhausted him but the essential work drove him on. His actions were different from other rescuers in that he was always on the spot personally, radiating self-confidence, and he was fearless.

Around Christmas things became chaotic with Arrow Cross men, some drunk, entering 'safe houses' and even legations and removing people. Wallenberg managed to get some protection from Hungarian police. On Christmas Eve all communication between Stockholm and Budapest ceased. On 28 December gas supplies ceased, on 30th the electricity was lost, on 3 January water supplies ceased.

Two children's homes were entered and some children shot; a Jewish hospital was entered and 28 young men killed. The terror culminated on New Year's Eve when Arrow Cross men started fighting among themselves. Wallenberg went about armed and changed houses frequently. The leading Zionist Otto Kolomy was killed. Eichmann managed to escape from the city before it was surrounded by the Russians. On 7 January Wallenberg and Giorgio Perlasca managed to get protection for Spanish Jews. But a safe house used by the legation was entered and the occupants beaten, robbed and about 180 shot on the banks of the Danube.

On 13 January the first Russian soldiers entered Budapest. A colonel greeted Wallenberg very politely and he was taken to the regimental HQ where he requested that he see Marshall Malinovsky who was in Debrecen in western Hungary. He wanted to secure protection for the Swedish safe houses and also present his plans for post-war Hungary.

Two days later the General Ghetto was liberated by Soviet soldiers. There had been rumours that the Ghetto was going to be annihilated before the Russians arrived either by a German air raid or by SS and Arrow Cross men. Szalai warned General Schmidhuber that Wallenberg had stated that if he did not prevent this he would be held responsible for murder. As a result the General ordered the SS and Arrow Cross to abandon their plans.

On 17 January Wallenberg prepared to leave Budapest to travel to see Marshall Malinovsky. He carried in his car jewels and gold belonging to Jews who had given them to him for safe keeping. His regular chauffeur and translator Vilmos Langfelder drove. However they never arrived at their destination for it emerged much later that a warrant had been issued in Moscow for Wallenberg's arrest. Both men were taken to Moscow and imprisoned in the Lubyanka prison. It seems that Wallenberg was suspected of being a German spy. He remained in Russian prisons until 1947 when it was later reported that he had died of a heart attack, although he may have been executed. So ended the life of one of the most remarkable and successful rescuers of the Nazi period.

Carl Lutz, Swiss Vice-Consul in charge of the interests of 14 belligerent nations including the USA and Britain was also a very successful diplomatic rescuer although a much more reserved man than Wallenburg. Before the Germans occupied Hungary he had helped 10,000 Jewish children and young people to emigrate to Palestine. When deportations began on 15 May 1944 he placed the staff of the Jewish Council for Palestine under diplomatic protection. A special relief organisation was created with a staff of 150 and his staff issued tens of thousands of 'protective letters'. He had permission to issue 8,000 so he never went above a printed number of 8,000 and simply repeated numbers.

70,000 Jews were liberated from the General Ghetto, 25,000 from the International Ghetto, and 25,000 were in hiding in homes, monasteries, convents and church cellars.

Bierman, John, *Righteous Gentile,* Penguin 1995

Fogelman, Eva, *Conscience and Courage: Rescuers of Jews during the Holocaust,* Anchor Books 1994

Jangfeldt, Bengt, *The Hero of Budapest,* I B Tauris, London 2014

Wallenburg, Raoul, *Letters and Dispatches 1924-1944,* Arcade Publishing, New York 1995

FRANZ JÄGERSTÄTTER (1907-1943)
AUSTRIAN CONSCIENTIOUS OBJECTOR

Franz Jägerstätter was born in 1907 in the small village of St Radegund, Upper Austria, whose population was entirely Roman Catholic. His mother, Rosalia Huber, was a maidservant and was unmarried but in 1917 she married Heinrich Jägerstätter who owned a farm. [Only 30 kms away is Brauman-am-Inn where Hitler was born in 1889, and the provincial capital of Linz is where Hitler spent his childhood, as did Eichmann.] Franz's maternal grandmother was exceptionally devout. Franz was above average at school but left at 14. As a young man he liked sports and was 'a bit wild' and daring. He brought the first motorcycle to the village. Gangs of youths were a feature of this district and Franz was an active member and involved himself in inter-gang fights. He was arrested and fined on one occasion.

As a young man he attended religious classes given by the priest but had the habit of asking awkward questions such as ones concerning the other children born to Mary the mother of Jesus. Some sort of dispute led him to be effectively exiled from the village for several years and he worked in iron mines during that time. He fathered a daughter, Hildegard, whose mother Theresia Auer was a farm maidservant in St Radegund. Franz's mother was opposed to marriage to Theresia but he did make maintenance payments for his daughter.

In 1936 he married Franziska a woman from a nearby village and they honeymooned in Rome, an unusual and significant choice. Jägerstatter had begun to change and his choice of bride, who was a very devout woman, indicated this. He began to sing hymns on his way to and from work; he gave up gambling at cards and he began to fast frequently.

His step-father handed over the farm to Franz when he married, as was the custom in this part of Austria. Although the family was quite poor he would often fill a rucksack with food and distribute it to those in greater need. Husband and wife made regular trips to a shrine in the area, often on motorbike. They were to have three daughters.

On 11 March 1938 the German army crossed the Austrian border and on 10 April a plebiscite overwhelmingly approved the Anschluss, the union with Germany. The Church leaders mostly approved although the Bishop of Linz, J M Gföllner, had expressed his opposition to Nazism from 1932. Franz's priest, Fr Karobath, himself an opponent of the Nazis, did not recommend a 'No' vote as it would have identified the opposition. Jägerstätter was the only one in the village to vote against the Anschluss. He also refused to take any government money such as family assistance or compensation for crops destroyed by bad weather. Criticism was made of his political stance but he was considered otherwise to be an excellent father and husband.

In 1940 he became sexton of his local church. He was strict in his duties, keeping people out of the sacristy if they didn't belong there and closing the doors of the church as soon as mass began. He also suggested to the young priest that he ought to preach more often about the sufferings of purgatory so that people might strive for greater perfection. He also criticised the funeral address for a soldier as praising military life. He refused to take payments from families of the deceased to arrange prayers for them. The other striking change was his very public expression of opposition to the Nazis. And he resigned from a peasants' union because it weakened its opposition to Nazism.

Jägerstätter underwent a brief period of military training but resolved that next time he would refuse. He joined the lay Third Order of St Francis. His friends, his mother and his parish priest tried to persuade him that it was pointless to refuse to serve in the army. He consulted several priests including his bishop but he remained firm that a Christian could not serve in an unjust war. His wife only reluctantly accepted his position.

On 1 March 1943 he refused to serve and was taken to the military prison at Linz. In prison he heard of a woman farmer who did not allow her children to serve in the Hitler Youth. He wrote to his wife and told her to speak the truth if anyone visited her. His letters had postscripts for the children. The letters make constant reference to the events of the Church calendar. He assured his wife that he was well but he did not encourage her to visit. The prison chaplain tried unsuccessfully to persuade him to serve in the army, especially for the sake of his family. Two of his cell-mates confirmed his convictions, sincerity and generosity.

In May he was moved to Berlin. He was still able to send letters to his wife but but less frequently (monthly). He was assigned an attorney called F L Feldmann who raised the question of why Catholic priests and bishops had not advised opposition to the regime. Jägerstätter replied that "they had not been given the grace". The proceedings were in a military court and he was asked to make a distinction between 'defence of the Fatherland' and any particular regime but he rejected this and would not compromise. He was however willing to serve as a paramedic in the army but was not given this option. The trial itself was brief and formal and the death sentence was mandatory. His monthly letter to his wife did not reveal the verdict. But Feldmann wrote to Fr Furthauer of St Radegund to help enlist the family to persuade Franz to change his mind. Fr Furthauer and Franz's wife went to Berlin to see him but Franz was resolute. Prison chaplain Dean Kreuzberg also visited him and told him of Fr Franz Reinisch who had been executed the previous year for "undermining military morale"; Jägerstätter was joyous at the news.

He was executed by guillotine on 9 August 1943; his ashes were later taken to St Radegund for burial. Jägerstätter believed firmly in the reality of Heaven (and Hell). He placed great store on honesty and truthfulness. He pointed out that the Catholic Church was opposed to Nazism up till it took power, demonstrating inconsistency. His beliefs were founded on the Bible and on the books of the saints which he read constantly.

There was controversy later over the inclusion of Jägerstätter's name on the village war memorial. Pastor Karobath insisted that it be there and a village meeting was held to consider it – his name was added at the end of the list of the war dead. The great majority of the villagers however considered his actions to be pointless and the result of excessive religious zeal. He was recognised by the Catholic Church in 2007 when he was beatified.

Zahn, Gordon, *In Solitary Witness: The Life and Death of Franz Jägerstätter,* Templegate Publishers 1986

Putz, Erna, *Franz Jägerstätter: A Shining Example in Dark Times,* Buchverlag Franz Steinmassi 2007

DENMARK – NATIONAL RESCUE OF JEWS 1940-45

Denmark had small military forces and could offer little armed resistance to Germany. The Government therefore negotiated a compromise whereby it would continue to run internal affairs, with a coalition government, but Germany would get farming and industrial supplies which suited the Germans well.

The country was occupied on 9 April 1940. Censorship of press, radio and external communications was accepted. However the Danish Ambassadors in Britain and USA declared themselves independent of the Government at home. Many Danish seamen joined the Allied forces. The Danish King Christian X continued his morning rides through Copenhagen. When a swastika flag was raised on a public building the King ordered its removal; when he said he would remove it personally if it was not done, the flag was lowered.

In December 1941 after an arson attack on the synagogue he sent a letter of sympathy to Rabbi Marcus Melchior. A few months earlier the Danish Foreign Minister had said to Hermann Goering: "There is no Jewish question in Denmark". Support for the Germans came from a small minority mostly in southern Jutland close to Germany. About 7,000 Danes joined the Waffen-SS but the Nazi leader, Dr Clausen, was not taken seriously by the Germans. So indulgent were the German occupiers that Werner Rings called it 'collaboration in reverse'. Parliamentary elections were even held as late as March 1943 with the Social Democrats receiving 44.6% of the vote and the National Socialists only 2%. Danish neutrality was accepted and the German authorities had to negotiate with the Danish Government over changes they wanted. The German officials and soldiers were instructed that Denmark was not an enemy country and Danes were to be treated well, especially Danish women, and they were not to get involved in political argument. One of the reasons for this relatively benign treatment was to counter the news of the mass killings of Poles which was spreading among the German population as soldiers from the eastern front told family and friends. SS General Werner Best, who had been Plenipotentiary from October 1942, even intervened, successfully, to save the lives of British airmen parachuted into Denmark and taken to Berlin.

When the war began to go against the German forces Danish discontent started to be expressed and illegal publications appeared and from 1943 the Danes resorted to sabotage. In the summer large strikes occurred in different towns and an end to cooperation with the Germans was an increasing demand. A state of emergency was declared on 29 August 1943 and General von Hanneken was given overall charge in place of Werner Best who had been considered too lenient. However Hitler quickly returned power to Best who now resolved to be tougher. Prominent Jews had been detained when the state of emergency was declared. The Danish army was also disarmed by the Wehrmacht and the soldiers interned.

Deportation of the Danish Jews began to be planned and German police battalions were brought in as the Wehrmacht was reluctant to participate. Raids on Jewish premises uncovered addresses of Jews. The round-up was planned for 1-2 October and now an attaché at the German Embassy, Georg F Duckwitz, tried to prevent it by going to Berlin but when this was unsuccessful he went to Sweden ostensibly on a trade mission but actually to see the Prime Minister. He was given an assurance that Sweden would receive Danish Jews so he returned and released the information about the round-up to a prominent MP Hans Hedoft who in turn told the Jewish leadership. This gave time for most Jews to be hidden by non-Jews in the towns and countryside in private homes, farms, churches, and even hospitals where they were disguised as patients or visitors, or simply hidden in rooms including the mortuary. Doctors, students and priests were particularly active and the Danish police and coast guards sometimes helped. Doctors organised collections and the Danish Medical Association gave a large donation. Even Wehrmacht soldiers sometimes looked the other way. Most Jews were then ferried to Sweden by fishing boats whose skippers were paid. Some of the escapees were caught and some died in accidents.

The acting chief rabbi Marcus Melchior and his family were put up in the vicarage of Hans Kildeby, 50 miles west of Copenhagen. The escape route took them to the Bishop's palace on Falster where about 150 people were fed and sheltered for a few days. Their escape experience now became almost farcical as the captain of the boat Melchior and others were put on did not have much sailing experience and he nearly landed them in a town full of German soldiers so the escapees took over the navigation themselves. The boat then ran out of fuel but Swedish fishermen saw them and came to the rescue. More than 7,000 were transported to freedom. Forty-five camps were set up in Sweden for the refugees and Danish schools were established in the major towns mostly funded by Danes.

The Germans managed to deport 481 Jews who were sent to Theresienstadt ghetto, north of Prague. The Danes were not transported to any of the death camps which was a promise obtained by Best from Eichmann. A commission from the Danish Foreign Ministry and Red Cross visited the camp on 23 June 1944 and saw the improved conditions especially arranged for their visit.

Although the state of emergency was called off after the move against the Jews, relations between the Germans and Danes deteriorated and resistance became more violent followed by German retaliation. During the last months of the war a Danish-Swedish-Norwegian rescue plan was put into operation and Scandinavian prisoners from German prisons and concentration camps were brought home. In April 1945 the Danes from Theresienstadt arrived by ferry at Malmo and this was followed by a great meeting in Stockholm. On 22 June the Copenhagen synagogue reopened presided over by the Chief Rabbi Friediger who had returned from Theresienstadt. The Jews in Sweden returned home and most integrated back into Danish society quite quickly.

In the 1950s Duckwitz served as German ambassador to Denmark and in 1971 he was named Righteous Among the Nations. The rescue of the Danish Jews, although relatively small in number, was the most successful in the occupied countries.

Bennett, Jeremy, 'The Resistance Against the German Occupation of Denmark 1940-45' in *Civilian Resistance as National Defence,* Edited by Adam Roberts, Pelican 1969

Straede, Therkel, *October 1943: the Rescue of the Danish Jews from Annihilation,* Royal Danish Ministry of Foreign Affairs 1993

Melchior, Marcus, *Darkness over Denmark* New English Library, London 1973

PROTESTS OF NON-JEWISH WIVES OF JEWS IN BERLIN 1943

The final roundup of Jews in Berlin began on 27 February 1943. There were still about 10,000 Jews in the city of which about 2,000 were married to non-Jewish spouses who had been exempted until then.

Social and legal pressures of the regime to abandon their spouses had not worked as about 93% remained married. Now all those wearing the Star of David were taken from their factories to collecting centres to be shipped to Auschwitz. The 2,000 were locked up at Rosenstrasse 2-4, an administrative centre of the Jewish community in the centre of Berlin. When the spouses, who were mostly women, realised that their spouses had not returned from work as usual they started to phone the factories and police. When they discovered where they had been taken they hurried to the Rosenstrasse and a substantial crowd gathered. The women then started shouting "Give us our husbands back!" The women threatened to break into the building. They then disbanded but agreed to gather early the next morning.

Although traffic was diverted to prevent growth of the crowds the numbers continued to grow to over 1000 with women coming for a period and then others arriving to replace them. The SS guards on a number of occasions in the next few days ordered the streets to be cleared or they would shoot. This caused the women to scatter into surrounding alleys and courtyards but they quickly gathered again to shout to their husbands and defy the armed guards. The headquarters of the Jewish Office of the Gestapo was just around the corner yet the order to fire was not given. Some ordinary Berliners watched the demonstration and word of it spread.

Then Goebbels decided to suspend the deportation for the present although the other 8,000 Jews were sent to their deaths. The Jewish spouses (more than 1,700) were released after a week.

They continued to live and work in Berlin officially registered with the police until the end of the war. However 25 of the group who were sent to work camps in Auschwitz were a few days later sworn to secrecy about their experiences at Auschwitz and sent to a 'work-education camp' near Berlin. Goebbels declared Berlin *judenfrei* (free of Jews) on 19 May although it was a lie.

On 21 May, Rolf Günther of the Gestapo replied to an enquiry from the German Police in Paris about what they should do with French Jews married to non-Jews. He said policy had not been determined yet and it depended on a solution in the Reich and especially Berlin. On the same day Himmler's deputy, Ernst Kaltenbrunner, ordered the release from concentration camps of all intermarried Jews except those interned on criminal charges. All other Jews in Germany were to be deported including hitherto exempted categories such as those in armament factories who had been considered irreplaceable. The order included: "I order expressly that Jewish intermarriage partners are in no case to be sent. ... In so far as Jewish intermarriage partners have been deported on general grounds they are to be successively released".

On 18 December 1943, Himmler ordered the deportation of Jews whose Aryan spouses had died or divorced them. However no such Jew was to be deported if they had a child or children who might stir up unrest as a result. The Nazis feared dissent on a wide scale and made concessions over other issues also such as labour mobilisation when strikes were threatened.

Stoltzfus, Nathan, 'Dissent in Nazi Germany' *The Atlantic Monthly* September 1992

A full account can be found in Stoltzfus, Nathan *Resistance of the Heart: Intermarriage and the Rosenstrasse Protest in Nazi Germany,* New York & London: W W Norton 1996

The Villagers of
Le Chambon-sur-Lignon, France

The village of Le Chambon is on a high plateau in SE France. The population at the beginning of the Second World War was around 3,000 and it was predominantly Protestant. A central figure in the village was an incomer, a Protestant Pastor, André Trocmé (b.1901). Trocmé came from a Huguenot family in Saint-Quentin in NE France but his mother was German. His father was a successful businessman in textiles. However there was tragedy in his childhood when his mother died in a car accident when being driven by his father. During part of the Great War Saint-Quentin was occupied by the German Army so the family moved to Belgium as refugees. André's experiences during the war had a profound effect on him and one in particular: a young soldier called Kindler was billeted on the family and to André's astonishment the soldier said he did not carry a weapon. He had become a Christian and so refused to carry a weapon but nevertheless was allowed to continue as a telegrapher. He spoke to André about nonviolence and Christianity. He was killed later in the war.

After the war André studied theology at the University of Paris, joined the Fellowship of Reconciliation and began work with trade unions in the Parisian suburbs. He then went to New York's Union Theological Seminary to study the Social Gospel then prevalent but he found it too secular. There he met an Italian student, Magda Grilli, who had been brought up a Catholic but did not now regard herself as either Catholic or Protestant. She also had mixed parentage as her mother was Russian. She was studying to be a social worker. André regarded America as too secular but Magda liked its freedom which contrasted with her life in Florence. Despite differences in outlook they returned to marry in France in 1926. Trocmé took parishes in industrial towns in northern France. Four children were born to them: Nelly, Jean-Pierre, Jacques and Daniel.

In 1934 they went south to Le Chambon-sur-Lignon on a plateau south of Lyon. It was a poor village which was largely cut off for much of the year because of severe weather. The parishioners of Trocmé's church were soon favourably impressed by his passionate preaching. A previous pastor in the village, Charles Guillon, who became the mayor in 1931 had been very international in outlook and travelled to many ecumenical conferences. He was later to be an active rescuer.

From early in the 20th century there was a tradition of bringing children in the summer to the Plateau Vivarais-Lignon (the latter was the river) as it was found to be good for their health. (Albert Camus, whose wife knew the area from spending holidays in her childhood, came here in 1942 for his tuberculosis.) An organisation was formed in 1910 to bring children to the plateau villages and so homes and hospitals were established staffed by doctors, medical students and social workers. It later became a popular tourist area, at least in summer, and by the start of the war there were nine hotels in Le Chambon alone. The rescuers associated with the internment camps began to send Jewish children to the villages of the Plateau.

Before the war Trocmé decided to start a school which would prepare students for the baccalauréats but also be free from red tape and would promote internationalism and peace. It was hoped to attract students and staff from abroad.

Edouard Theis, a friend from University of Paris days and also a pacifist was invited to establish the school. He taught Latin and Greek and French and also became part-time pastor. In 1937 the Ecole Nouvelle Cévenol opened with four teachers and 18 students but it grew rapidly. They did not at first have a science teacher so the students were sent for that to the public boys' school headed by Roger Darcissac. Both teachers and students were of many nationalities, especially eastern European, but also an Englishwoman, Gladys Maber. A good few students and staff were Jewish. Some of the staff were outstanding scholars or scientists who, as Jews, had lost their positions.

After the German occupation of the north of France and the

formation of the Vichy regime schools reopened after the 1940 summer vacation under Vichy control. This meant giving the Nazi salute to the French flag every morning. Some students of the school formed a semi-circle around a teacher who was a supporter of Pétain but as time went on fewer and fewer students did so and within a few weeks the ceremony disappeared completely. A few weeks later all the staff of Cévenol refused to sign an oath of loyalty to Pétain.

A conflict with the mayor occurred when he instructed the pastor to have the bells of the Protestant church (actually called a temple) rung to celebrate the founding by Pétain on 1 August 1941 of the Legion of Veterans. This Legion later became the Malice, equivalent to the SS. The small Catholic Church rang its bell but not the temple. In fact the custodian who was a Darbyste woman (they were very strict Protestants) had been approached by two women visitors to ring the bell but she refused and barred their way to the bell tower.

In the summer of 1942 the Minister of Youth, Georges Lamirand, visited Le Chambon but was surprised at the lack of enthusiasm for his visit and the absence of welcoming crowds. A dozen older students from Cévenol took the opportunity of his visit to hand the Minister a letter protesting at the arrest of Jews in Paris and saying that they had Jews among their students and would not surrender them if demanded. The Minister quickly left. Prefect Bach was furious and blamed Trocmé for this and threatened not just Jews who had settled in the village but the pastor himself.

Some weeks later the police chief of Haute-Loire region arrived with buses in the square of the village and summoned Trocmé to demand the names of Jews in the village. Trocmé replied that he did not know names (they had adopted false names) and in any case he would not give their names even if he did know them. The pastor then called the Boy Scouts and Bible Class leaders and sent them to warn those hiding in farm houses. The Jews scattered to the woods and further afield. The church was full on Sunday while the police did searches and Trocmé and Theis urged their people to stand by their refugees no matter what. As time went on many Vichy police helped the Jews by ignoring orders and giving warnings.

The sheltering of Jews had begun in the winter 1940-41 when a starving Jewish woman knocked on the presbytery door of Le Chambon and Magda let her in. The mayor refused to help get her false papers. The woman's shoes had been put in the oven to dry them and they got accidentally burnt so Magda searched the village and found a pair and so the next morning the woman was able to leave. Magda knew of a Catholic family who would help hide her. Later, another German Jew appeared and this time Magda went to the French wife of a French rabbi staying in Le Chambon but was shocked to find she would not help as she blamed foreign Jews for the plight of French Jews. Although the refugees had to be helped it meant lying at times – a difficult moral issue for the Christians. But the rescuers did not deny the fact that Jews were hiding in the village only that they would not reveal them. Later in the winter Trocmé went to Marseilles where the office of the American Friends Service Committee was located. He already had the support of his church council. The Quakers were helping bring supplies to internment camps at Gurs and Argeles. They suggested financing one house of refuge in the village. A different position was taken by the Reformed Church of which Trocmé was a member and a high ranking official was sent to persuade him to give up helping Jews, something he firmly refused to do and had the support of his family in that.

At the time of the German occupation of the south there were 160 central European refugees in six houses in Le Chambon. The safe houses were financed by Quakers, American Congregationalists, the World Council of Churches and neutral governments such as Sweden and Switzerland. The Farm School which was located far into the countryside was funded by Switzerland. Another, Flowery Hill, sheltered people intending to cross the mountains to Switzerland with the help of Cimade. Edouard Theis became one of the guides late in the war when he was fleeing from the Gestapo. There were also the boarding houses in the village itself – one was that of Madame Eyraud who usually had 14 boys staying. Her husband was in the Resistance. There were a number of other *pensions* in the village and also family homes who took Jews. There were a few Darbystes among the rescuers as they were sympathetic to Jews because of their love of the Old Testament. Some of the families on the outskirts kept refugees for years. The Cévenol School was an important hiding place for both pupils and adults. Being outside the village in wooded countryside to the north meant that it was ideal for hiding. It was well run and never drew the attention of the security people.

Trocmé in particular did not get on well with Le Maquis who, apart from using violence, sometimes stole their bicycles, cars and other goods to use or sell. The Secret Army of General de Gaulle was less troublesome and locally they were led by a Jew from Marseilles who got on well with Trocmé although they differed over the issue of violence. It was not only Jews who hid in Le Chambon. There were Spanish Republicans who were the first to appear, then anti-Nazi Germans, then young Frenchmen escaping forced labour in Germany, but Jews were the largest group, about 2,500 during the war. One worked as a doctor in the practice of Le Forestier, some with the Red Cross, some teaching in school. French Jews were naturally easier to hide than foreign. There was little joint organisation in the village except for identity cards. Oscar Rosowsky, a young Russian Jew, was very useful in that respect. He had moved with his parents and two brothers from Riga to Berlin and then to Nice. One day his mother was arrested because she had false ID papers so he forged another and sent it to Rivesaltes and to his astonishment she was released. Hearing of the villages on the Plateau he went to Fay-le-Froid and his mother followed. He then went to Le Chambon where he developed his skill at producing documents.

On 13 February 1943 two French policemen including Major

Silvani, Chief of Haute Loire, arrived in Le Chambon. Only Magda was at home as André was doing visits in the parish. Visits included the leaders of the 13 youth groups or *responsables* who were important in the nonviolent resistance. Magda invited the policemen in and after two hours her husband arrived home. Silvani then told him he was arrested. As it was dinner time Magda invited the police to eat. When the villagers heard of the arrest they came to say farewell and brought gifts with them. Silvani was upset by such a display. As Trocmé left with the police the villagers lined the streets and sang *A mighty fortress is our Lord*. The police then went to arrest Theis and Darcissac, the latter being a copier of false documents. Darcissac had fled but his wife persuaded him to surrender and the three were taken to Le Puy. (In 1955 Trocmé wrote a letter that restored Silvani to favour with the French Government.)

The three were interned in Saint-Paul d'Eyjeaux near Limoges. The inmates already there looked starved. They were mostly Communists with some Catholics who were opposed to the regime. The Communists did not like the new prisoners' nonviolent beliefs. While there they heard of the defeat of the Germans at Stalingrad but the three friends viewed this in a mixed way. With time the other prisoners came to respect their position and what they had done in Le Chambon. To the surprise of the other prisoners Magda and Darcissac's son and others brought a variety of gifts, mainly food, in spite of the village being poor. The three also got permission to hold services and discussions which were attended by non-Christians too. After a month the three were offered release but on condition that they sign a paper saying they would obey the orders of the Government. Because Darcissac was head of a public school he had already signed such a document and could be released but the other two would not sign so Darcissac asked to remain, but he was not allowed to do so. The Communists thought they were fools, however the next morning the two were released on the orders of Prime Minister Laval, reason unknown. A few days later the inmates were deported to camps in Poland and salt mines in Silesia and very few survived to the end of the war.

In mid-summer 1943 Commissioner Praly, who had been sent a year earlier by the Vichy regime to identify the Jews and the few Maquis in and around the village, was shot. In July a member of the Maquis told Trocmé that the Gestapo had ordered him to be killed by a hit-and-run driver. Trocmé decided to leave and all the family left Le Chambon on bicycles. Magda had made a new identity for him and he now went off on his own and entered the presbytery of Lamastre. The pastor was on holiday but when he returned he asked Trocmé to leave. A friend with a car took him to a house on a hill with a good view of approaching vehicles and the Gestapo lost his trail. He moved house a couple of times but when he heard that his son Jacques was unhappy because of his father's absence he invited Jacques to come and stay with him. He undertook his son's education with the help of a Jew who lived nearby and who taught mathematics. It was one of the happiest periods of their lives. But on a visit to Lyon for an important meeting they both had a very narrow escape from capture by German soldiers because Trocmé had a false passport and had decided he would not lie about his name if asked – he was not asked.

André's cousin Daniel Trocmé moved from teaching in his father's famous school to Le Chambon to supervise the House of the Rocks. He was in his mid-20s and had a weak heart but he "worked like a madman" as Magda said of him. On 29 June 1943 the Rocks was raided by the Germans. When Magda heard from one of the girls that Daniel had been arrested she rushed to the House of the Rocks. She walked into the building, being mistaken for a maid because she still had her apron on, and sat in the kitchen as the Gestapo did not know who she was. They began interrogating students and Daniel. After a while the students were given something to eat and Magda helped and thus got the chance to speak to them and to Daniel. Daniel told her that a few weeks earlier one of the boys – a refugee from Spain called Pepito – had saved a German soldier from drowning in the

Lignon and he requested Magda to go to the German Army HQ and plead for their release because of this action.

She managed to get there and persuaded two German officers to come with her, even getting bicycles for them from two women she knew. Pepito was released after the soldiers spoke to the Gestapo men but the others were put into a bus. Much later when one of the students returned to Le Chambon they learned that Daniel had been sent to Maidanek in eastern Poland where he was gassed on 4 April 1944. The Germans believed he must be Jewish because of his sympathy for Jews.

Shortly after the Normandy invasion on 6 June 1944 Trocmé and his son were able to return home where they were greeted joyously by the villagers. While Trocmé had been away Darcissac continued to produce false documents and gave shelter to the Maquis in his school. Theis became a rescuer with Cimade (one of the few men) who took refugees to Switzerland and he continued to do so for a year. Trocmé now discovered that many of the Cévenol school students had joined the Maquis. Meanwhile Magda and her friend Simone Mairesse had been coping with even more refugees and the houses of refuge were always full and the Cimade was busier than ever. When the Allies landed in the south of France on 15 August 1944 the battle of France was in its last weeks. Some German prisoners were massacred by the Maquis. Trocmé preached to German prisoners as well as French Maquis but neither was convinced of the way of nonviolence.

After the Normandy invasion the German army became more dangerous. One day news came that the Germans were approaching Le Chambon from the east and it was decided to evacuate the population. Everyone moved to farmhouses. In the evening Trocmé came to the village square and saw Dr Roger Le Forestier, an incomer to the village like the pastor, and a group of Maquis arguing as they wanted his ambulance to transport troops which he refused. Trocmé defended the doctor's stance.

Le Forestier then drove to Le Puy to try to get two Maquisards released from prison. But when he returned to his car some Gestapo men were there and they beat him up because they had found a gun in the car which had been hidden there by two Maquisards he had given a lift to. He was charged with a plot against the German army but apparently volunteered to go to Germany to serve the German people as a doctor.

After the liberation of France Le Forestier's young wife Danielle searched for her husband and found that he had been shot along with 120 prisoners on the orders of local SS chief Klaus Barbie. He could have escaped on the journey from Le Puy to Lyons (as some did) but he refused having given his word that he would go to Germany.

In September French troops liberated Le Chambon. Soon the refugees left followed by the Maquis as they joined the army further north. Now the village had to build a new life. André turned to reviving the Cévenol School and would visit the USA to raise funds. The school/college continues to flourish today taking both local children and students from abroad. He began to lecture for the Fellowship of Reconciliation and became its European Secretary. He later became pastor of Saint-Gervais in Geneva.

How many Jews and others were saved by the actions of the villagers of the Plateau is impossible to know but it was probably a few thousand.

Hallie, Philip, *Lest Innocent Blood be Shed,* Harper Perennial 1994

Fogelman, Eva, *Conscience and Courage: Rescuers of Jews During the Holocaust*, Anchor Books 1995

Moorehead, Caroline, *Village of Secrets: Defying the Nazis in Vichy France*, Chatto & Windus 2014

GENERAL RESISTANCE IN NORWAY 1940-45

At the beginning of the invasion on 9 April 1940 German plans were thrown into confusion as the ship carrying the political and military general staff was sunk by the Norwegians. In this situation the Norwegian fascist Vidkun Quisling announced a new government of National Unity (Nasjonal Samling or NS) but some of the ministers he named refused to serve and most of the civil servants closed their offices. With Quisling unable to get sufficient support he was dismissed by the invaders, and the Germans negotiated with the Supreme Court members.

The Norwegian resistance continued till 7 June with some help from British forces. According to Myrtle Wright, a British Quaker who found herself trapped in Norway on the outbreak of war, the British troops gave an unfavourable impression as some of them looted Norwegian property in contrast to the Germans who were better disciplined. When some British soldiers were cut off from the main body another Quaker woman, Ingeborg Sletten, led them nearly 100 miles to the Swedish border. On the surrender of the armed forces, King Haakon and the Government left for London on a British ship which also carried hundreds of Norwegian troops and funds from the Bank of Norway. This meant that the legitimate political institutions continued to exist to an extent even if not for the time being in the homeland.

The trade unions allowed their elected leaders to be replaced by German nominees fearing that they would be disbanded if they resisted. The Germans demanded that Parliament (Storting) be recalled on 13 June to depose the King and arrange for new elections. A small body (about 6 individuals) called the Presidentskap reluctantly asked for the King's resignation but he replied with a refusal on 3 July. On 25 September Reichcommisar Joseph Terboven dissolved the Parliament and all political parties except the NS headed by Vidkun Quisling although the NS only had about 2% support in the country. When Germany invaded Russia in June 1940 Terboven appealed for a Norwegian legion of 10,000 but fewer than 1,000 volunteered. This administration continued until 1 February 1942 when Quisling was allowed to take office as Minister-President.

Resistance took some time to develop and was two-fold – military (Milorg) and civilian (Sivorg). However many existing organisations adapted to an occupation situation and played an important role. Sivorg and Milorg were largely separate but did maintain regular contact from March 1943. During the first phase, until summer 1941, discontent was unorganised and took the form of street demonstrations, booing, heckling, as well as giving misleading directions and refusing to acknowledge the presence of a German. Civil servants were divided in their reactions, some resigned their posts, some collaborated, some remained on duty hoping to defend Norway's interests. As elsewhere the nonviolent resistance was largely pragmatic but a small number of pacifists took it up because of their ethical belief. Myrtle Wright managed to give some talks to school classes and Quaker groups on Gandhian nonviolence.

In the winter of 1940-41 civilian resistance began to be organised. There were public protests against random arrests; against the use of torture in interrogations; against violence used by the Hird (the Norwegian equivalent of the SS); against compulsory membership of Nasjonal Samling (NS) for civil service entrance; and against the abolition of national and local elections.

The Norwegian Supreme Court resigned on 21 December 1940 in protest against the Reichcommissar's declaration that it had no right to declare 'laws' unconstitutional. In May 1941, 43 organisations representing about three-quarters of a million members sent a letter to the Reichscommissar objecting that decrees were being issued that violated international law and Norwegian law. Some trade unions joined the protest after pressure from rank and file members. Terboven reacted by arresting some of the signatories and dissolving all of the organisations. Although the men were released a refusal of a pay increase and cancellation of the milk allowance in factories provoked a strike in September and a state of emergency was declared. Two of the men were shot and many arrested and Quisling appointees took control of the unions.

The Athletics Association stopped activities when there was an attempt to impose commissioners upon them and no skiing competitions or other sporting events took place during the occupation. In April 1941 the Medical Association voted 32 to 2 against amalgamating with the NS Guild of Health. Out of 2,100 members only about 100 eventually joined the Guild. On 25 April 1941 Dr Gjessing, a psychiatrist, was dismissed from the position of Director of a large mental hospital resulting in 150 medical staff protesting, as did the Bishop and the Rektor of Oslo University. On 25 June Dr Gjessing was reinstated by Terboven and the Hird were told not to interfere. Students boycotted Nazi lectures and the Nazi students' union. In the students' union 70-year-old Dr Sharffenberg called for loyalty to the king and met with tumultuous applause. A few days later he was imprisoned and the students' union was dissolved on 11 October. Professor Seip, the Rektor, refused to comply with a new board of examiners in the law faculty and in September 1941 he was dismissed and sent to Sachsenhausen concentration camp which he managed to survive. Trade unions however showed less desire to resist the New Order – although there was a strike in September 1941 over wage levels – and factories and transport continued to function.

Communications were vital for the resistance but radio sets were confiscated throughout the country from September 1941 except for members of the NS. Fortunately not all were surrendered or discovered and some were smuggled in from Sweden and Britain. Much of the communication was done by the underground press which concentrated on conveying news and especially on the progress of the war, which in turn depended on reports by the BBC. The other main topic of the press was news of acts of resistance, and repressive acts of the regime. It was not easy to keep the news impartial and the press was propagandistic. Nor were the producers of the papers in general pacifists and they often armed themselves.

There was some pacifist influence. Ole Olden, Rektor of St Swithen's School in Stavanger, and a Quaker pacifist, spent 8 months in Grini concentration camp outside Oslo. In spring 1941 Ingebord Ljusnes, a member of the Women's International League for Peace and Freedom, who was a photographer, refused to take pictures of German officers, and after she had made a derogatory remark she was sentenced to a year in prison. Myrtle Wright herself was twice summoned to the Gestapo headquarters at Victoria Terrace where she was interrogated by Gestapo officer Witteg who forbad her to have any further contact with students. The couple who gave her a home while she was in Norway, Diderich and Sigrid Lund, were members of the War Resisters' International. Diderich was an engineer who travelled around the country for his professional work and this was a useful cover for his work in the nonviolent underground. Eventually he was warned of risk of arrest and escaped to Sweden in 1944.

Noncooperation was used by several occupational groups but most notably by the teachers. In the Autumn of 1940 control of education was passed to Quisling. A document was drawn up which all teachers had to sign committing them to promote the New Order. To refuse to sign was to mean immediate dismissal. The teachers drafted a counter declaration which read: "In connection with the communication which has been received, I herewith declare that I shall remain faithful to my vocation as a teacher and to my conscience, and that on this basis I shall continue to follow such instructions for my work as are lawfully given by my superiors". [Skodvin p.172]

In the summer of 1941 the teachers' organisation was taken over by the Nazis and the teachers left and formed their own underground branches. By the autumn a policy had been worked out with four main points:

1. Refuse all demands to join the NS or make declarations of loyalty to it.
2. Reject all attempts to introduce NS propaganda in schools.
3. Refuse all orders from unauthorised quarters.
4. Do not cooperate in any way with the NS youth organisation.

(Skodvin p.173)

On 5 February 1942, a few days after he had taken office, Quisling proclaimed the law creating the Norwegian Teachers' Union. This was intended to be the beginning of the creation of a corporate state. A youth organisation was also made compulsory for those aged 10-18. New textbooks were being prepared also so that teachers could teach the new ideology. On 12 February teachers from primary and secondary schools met secretly in Oslo and decided to send out their own declaration repudiating the official directives. They decided that every teacher should be encouraged to send their own objection to the Ministry around 20 February. One teacher active in the resistance had the message passed on to him in a matchbox at a railway station. In the densely populated areas where they could be easily reached, more than 90% of teachers sent letters. Altogether about 10,000 out of 14,000 sent letters. Magne Jensen who was the main drafter of the letters said after the war: the letters "created the feeling of solidarity at a rather early stage, which was so necessary for civilian combat. They broke the feeling of individual isolation, the dread of remaining alone, which was the main weapon of Nazi terror". [Semelin p.70] 150 university teachers posted their objection to the Quisling Youth Front on the same day.

On 23 February the Ministry warned that teachers who had not withdrawn their declarations before 1 March would be dismissed. The teachers were instructed by their own organisations to avoid anything that could be called a strike and should continue working. The ministry then announced that schools were to be closed 'due to the fuel shortage' for a month. This caused protests from parents who now sent letters saying: "I do not want my children to take part in the NS youth organisation as the plans that have been drawn up for it violate my conscience". [Skodvin p.175] This was sent by more than 100,000 parents who gave their names and addresses.

The authorities responded by drawing up a list of teachers to be arrested – 1000, all men, to be selected. Somewhat controversially Norwegian police took part in the arrests. Some of the men were sent to the concentration camp at Falstad, others to a camp at Jorstadmoen and put on a starvation diet and given hard labour in the hope of breaking their will to resist. Running and crawling in the snow was a common treatment. Only 32 out of 687 gave in to pressure. When being transported between camps word often got around and schoolchildren gathered at the stations the train was passing through and sang. The teachers' families received payments during their detention, in part from the Government-in-Exile and in part from parents and supporters. Then in April and May about 650 were sent to the Arctic Circle, being transported by ship for 13 days, crammed into too small a space, to Kirkenes where they were forced to work alongside Russian prisoners of war unloading ships cargo in terrible conditions. However even before some of the teachers had been transported to Kirkenes the schools were reopened. The teachers read a statement to their pupils making it clear that they would not be complying with the regime's aims. In a speech at a high school in Stabekk in May 1942 Quisling declared angrily: "You teachers have destroyed everything for me". All the teachers at the school were arrested. But the saying by Quisling became a slogan of the resistance.

Eventually in August about 150 of the teachers in Kirkenes who were in poor health signed a document with the approval of the others agreeing to join the new teachers' organisation (which never came into being). Then in September, 100 were released without signing anything. It was November before the remaining 400 who had refused to compromise were released and they were met at the railway station by crowds and put up in the best hotels. The teachers' resistance had been followed by the whole population for the eight months of their ordeal. After further difficulties for Quisling's plan Hitler ordered the abandonment of the attempt to set up a Corporate State.

The Christian clergy also resisted Nazi encroachment on their sphere. On 15 January 1941 a letter from all seven bishops of the Lutheran Church was sent to the Ministry of Church and Education condemning violence by the Hird. They protested also about a new decree abolishing the clergy's right not to reveal to the police information acquired in the course of pastoral work. Not receiving a satisfactory reply the letter was sent as a pastoral letter to the congregations. 50,000 copies were printed.

The official Ministry planned to hold a mass in the Cathedral in Trondheim to celebrate the inauguration of Quisling's National Government. Only a handful of people attended this but in contrast a service later in the day called by the Dean attracted thousands and when the police closed the doors of the cathedral thousands stood in extremely cold weather singing hymns. The next day the Dean was dismissed but this was followed by the resignation of the bishops who disassociated themselves from the State while intending to continue their work. The Ministry then officially dismissed the Bishop of Oslo, Eivind Berggrav.

On Easter Sunday, 5 April 1942, it was announced in the churches that the clergy were renouncing their official posts, and hence their salaries, while continuing their pastoral duties. Till the end of the war there was no state church in the country although attempts were made to ordain 'Quisling' bishops and deans. The clergy were harassed and some imprisoned and two died in concentration camps.

By the end of 1942 around 100 Norwegians had been executed, 7,000 were in concentration camps and 1,000 had been deported to Poland. Since July 1941 all Norwegians had been liable to undertake war work of some nature but wages were relatively high for such work so there was no difficulty getting the numbers required. But by 1943 war work pay did not exceed other work so compulsory registration was introduced. However many did not register or if registered were often not to be found as they were in hiding. The Oslo Registration Office holding records of the entire country was also set on fire. Even extra powers for the police and special courts did not produce enough workers for the occupying power.

In February 1943 men aged 18-55 and women aged 21-40 were called up for forced labour. Unlike some of the professions the resistance by students was not strong. In addition about 100,000 Norwegians worked voluntarily for the Germans due to good pay rates. In contrast, some police refused to arrest conscripts who did not turn up for duty and consequently some police were imprisoned and one shot. 150 police were imprisoned in Grini for refusing to sign a declaration.

There were even fewer Jews in Norway than in Denmark, about 1,700, and more than half escaped to Sweden. On 1 September 1942 Chief Rabbi Samuel of Oslo and 10 other Jews were arrested. On 25 October there was a general arrest of Jewish men but many were hidden. On 25 November Jewish men and women were arrested, some being imprisoned and some transported immediately, but many escaped the arrests due to warnings from the police. On 24 February 1943 all Jews in Bredvedt prison were shipped to Auschwitz; only 12 of around 700 survived the war.

The Norwegian population displayed a high degree of solidarity during the occupation. For example the black market was run on a more democratic basis than in most countries. Although foodstuffs were supposed to be handed over to the occupiers for distribution rather a lot was not. These amounts were sold at only a slightly higher level than the official stores and much was bought by employers for their workforce or by people who were looking after those in hiding. Almost no profit was made from this.

Skodvin, Magne, 'Norwegian Nonviolent Resistance during the German Occupation' in *Civilian Resistance as a National Defence,* Edited by Adam Roberts, Penguin 1969

Wright, Myrtle, *Norwegian Diary 1940-45,* Friends Peace and International Committee 1974

Sharp, Gene, *Tyranny Could not Quell Them,* Peace News Publications 1958

Irena Sendlerowa
and other Polish rescuers

Irena Sendlerowa (1910-2008) was the daughter of a physician who from childhood was pro-Jewish although the family were Catholic. At Warsaw University she openly opposed the bench-ghetto system introduced in 1935 which compelled Jewish students to sit in designated seats at lectures. This led to her being suspended from university for 3 years.

She became a social worker and from the beginning of the occupation she began to help Jews by making up, with helpers, over 3,000 false documents. She joined the children's section of Zegota, the Council to Aid Jews, when it formed. Helping Jews was particularly dangerous in Poland as the penalty was death.

In 1942, she entered the ghetto to check for typhus. She had access as she was employed by the Social Welfare Department of Warsaw and had special permission but she wore a Star of David on these occasions, partly as solidarity and partly because it made access to people easier. She then arranged to smuggle children out of the ghetto with the help of about 20 others such as plumbers and electricians who also had access to the ghetto. The children were hidden in boxes, suitcases and trolleys and when safely out were placed with Polish families, with priests, and with the Warsaw orphanage of Sisters of the Family of Mary. Their names, and adopted names, were written on pieces of paper which were put in jars and buried in neighbours' gardens so that the children might be reunited with their parents in the future.

Irena Sendlerowa was arrested in 1943. She was then tortured but revealed no names and was sentenced to death. She survived through Zegota agents bribing a German officer being left in a forest with her arms and legs broken but she lived and went into hiding and when she recovered her health she took up work for Jewish children again. After the war she dug up the jars but most of the parents had been killed in Treblinka. She and her collaborators had saved about 1,500 Jewish children.

After the war she was imprisoned by the Communist Government because of her links to the Home Army and had a miscarriage in prison. Later her children were denied the right to study at university because of their mother's record.

What she had done during the occupation was eventually recognised and she was given many international awards.

Henryk Slawick came from a poor peasant family and joined the pre-war Polish army and then served as a police officer in Silesia until 1939. He was also a member of the Polish Socialist Party. On the invasion of Poland he joined the Krakow Army to fight the Germans but when their unit retreated over the Hungarian border he was placed in a refugee camp. However being fluent in German he was taken to Budapest where he helped set up a committee to help Polish refugees. He aided Jews by obtaining forged passports and priests helped by issuing false birth certificates. Slawick also set up an orphanage for Jewish children but disguised it as a Catholic school. He also joined the Polish Government-in-Exile. When Germany invaded Hungary he urged the refugees to leave the country and most escaped but not himself. The Gestapo tortured him and then sent him to Mauthausen where he was shot in August 1944. He had helped rescue about 30,000 Polish refugees, about 5,000 of them Jews.

Many Polish clergy were rescuers and at least 189 convents hid about 1,500 Jewish children mainly in the Warsaw district. Nuns themselves were persecuted from October 1939 and many went into hiding.

An individual rescuer was Stanislawa Dawidziak, a young factory worker with a one room flat shared with her waiter husband and a teenage brother. In 1943 at her husband's request she took in a Jewish woman, Irena, for one night. This extended to weeks until her husband refused to risk his life any longer for the woman but as Stanislawa would not ask Irena to leave, her husband left her. Later Stanislawa, who had been pregnant, gave birth to a baby boy. The Polish policeman, Kaminski, who had brought Irena continued to bring food and they survived.

Another case was of a rescuer, Antonina (Tonia) Sivak, who worked as a maid in Lwow serving a family of a German officer. One day she met another maid who was Jewish, Rivka Hollander, who was alone in Lwow as her husband was in the Russian Army. They became friends and Rivka asked Tonia to help get her sister out of a camp. She offered Tonia a diamond ring for this help. However they did not succeed and Tonia returned the ring although she did not need to. In 1942 all Jews in Lwow were ordered to move to the ghetto but Tonia hid Rivka in the apartment. This lasted three years. As danger increased Rivka went into the countryside but she returned and Tonia rented a room for her. At the end of the war Rivka was reunited with her husband.

Zygmunt Rytel was born in 1922 in the small town of Krzemienice to a Catholic family. About half of the population was Jewish so it is not surprising that he had Jewish friends at school. He regarded himself as an individualist who stood up for things that he believed in. After school he applied for an engineering course but then after the German invasion he turned to writing and journalism and joined the Polish Socialist Party. Initially he defended those Polish individuals who were regarded as the elite which the Germans wanted to eliminate, such as artists and intellectuals. At the beginning of the war his brother was shot by a German officer. He was himself, at only 18, arrested and sent to the general concentration camp of Auschwitz for eight months. From 1943 he concentrated on helping Jews who he now saw were the most in need. He came to Warsaw and was given a small flat by the Socialist Party who asked him to become a document forger to replace one who had been caught. He then started to arrange safe houses for those sought by the Germans. He joined Zegota who were helping particularly Jews who tried to pass as non-Jews. Zygmont distributed funds from the Government-in-Exile and other sources. He transported Jews and others to other towns and he was also persuaded to make films as historical documents. He found that older people were better at hiding others for lengthy periods as they were more patient than the young who were better at more adventurous activities. He saved at least 100 individuals.

Alexander Roslan was born near Bialystok and he and his brothers worked their farm after their father was killed in the First World War. Their mother and grandmother often sheltered and fed wandering Gypsies although they were not a particularly religious family. They began to worry that the farm would be taken over by the Russians so they sold it and divided the proceeds and Alex, now married to Mela with two children, Jurek and Mary, bought a fabric shop in

Bialystok where he did a lot of trade with Jews. When the Russians occupied eastern Poland in 1939 the family fled to Warsaw where Alex worked in the black market. Out of curiosity, he was smuggled into the ghetto and was horrified at what he saw.

He decided to take in a Jewish child and a friend brought him a 13-year-old boy, Jacob Gutgelt, who was Jewish in appearance. He was already feeding two Catholic children, one of whom was severely disabled. He built a false wall in a cupboard where Jacob could hide in times of danger. In fact they were twice inspected by the Gestapo during which the children played noisily to hide any sound Jacob might make. Alex also gave the Germans alcohol to divert them from a thorough inspection. The family moved to the suburbs to be safer but Alex was now further from his customers. Jacob tutored Mary in mathematics and reading. But then they were asked by the underground to take in Jacob's brother, Sholom. Mela was not at all happy about this increased risk but Sholom was accepted and found to be severely undernourished. Two months later Sholom developed scarlet fever which spread to Jurek. Fortunately the local doctor could be trusted but Jurek needed to be sent to hospital. Jurek did an extraordinary thing – he took only half his medicine and hid the rest and also took notes about his treatment and gave them to his mother when she visited asking her to treat Shalom.

Sadlly, Shalom did not recover. This led to another problem – where to bury the body. At night with the help of the crippled boy he buried Shalom in the earthen basement of the house. Next, Jacob developed a severe fever. He went to a trusted doctor who asked for money to bribe nurses but Alex had none; so he now sold the house for cash but Mela became hysterical when she was told. They had now to live in a one room apartment but he took Jacob to the clinic and within a few days he was able to come home. Being now in the centre of Warsaw again Alex had opportunities to trade on the back market which he did successfully and soon they were able to move to a larger flat. But now Alex was approached to take

Jacob's seven-year-old brother which they did. But Alex's illegal trading led to him being arrested and imprisoned. Now it was Mela who came to his aid by bribing prison staff and he was released but not the men he had bought from. Before anything further could be done the Warsaw Uprising began and in the following weeks everyone lived in basements including Jacob but now fortunately there was no one to complain to about a free Jew. But the Uprising brought its own tragedy to the Roslans when a stray bullet killed Jurek when he went to fetch water. The Uprising was suppressed and Warsaw was emptied by the Germans leaving people to roam the countryside including the Roslans who had the added problem of Jacob and the possibility of betrayal. Soon the Russians arrived and at least their lives were relatively safe although the survivors had all been greatly traumatised.

Jan Karski was born in Lodz in 1914 to a Catholic family. After university he joined the Polish Foreign Service and in 1939 became an officer in the Polish army. He was taken prisoner by the Russians but escaped and joined the Home Army (AK) in Warsaw. He became an emissary and in 1940 set out for France where the Polish Government-in-Exile was located. He included in his reports one about life in Poland under German and Soviet occupation. He advised a common front of Poles and Jews against the occupiers.

He returned to Poland but on a second mission was arrested by the Gestapo in Slovakia. He was tortured and tried to commit suicide but was rescued by a Polish commando group. Giving priority to the situation of the Jews, he met with Jewish leaders and also obtained first hand experience of their plight by being smuggled into the Warsaw ghetto and a transit camp. Abroad he met with Roosevelt, Churchill and other leaders including the Polish-Jewish leader of the socialist Bund, Szmuel Zygielbojm, who had escaped from Poland to London. There was to be disappointment as the Allied leaders gave no material support to the Jews and Zygielbojm committed suicide in protest. Karski summarised his belief: "We hear it said that the Jews were abandoned by governments, social structures, church hierarchies, but not by ordinary men and women." [Tec, p.186]

Karski was unable to return to Poland but he continued to spread knowledge of the Jews under Nazism by giving many lectures in the USA and writing a book on the subject. He estimated that about half a million Jews in Europe had been helped by non-Jews from all walks of life. Later in life Karski married Pola Nirenska, a dancer and choreographer, who was Jewish.

Thousands of Poles have been recognised by Yad Vashem as Righteous for saving Jews, more than any other nation.

Gilbert, Martin, *The Righteous: The Unsung Heroes of the Holocaust,* Black Swan 2002

Tec, Nechama, *Resistance,* Oxford University Press 2013

Eva Fogelman, *Conscience and Courage,* Books 1995

DUTCH RESCUERS

The family of Anne Frank was one of a great many hidden by Dutch rescuers.

Theresa Weerstra, mother of three, accepted a 4-year-old Jewish girl who was brought to her by a friend while her husband was at work. She persuaded him that it was a Christian thing to do and this led in time to them sheltering as part of a network an astounding 450 people who included Jews, Allied pilots and Dutch men avoiding labour conscription. When one of the women they were hiding became pregnant Theresa pretended to be pregnant herself and padded out her clothes appropriately so that when the child was born she could pass it as her own.

Joop Westerweel and his wife Will were Montessori teachers in Rotterdam with a large following of students and teachers. When they returned from holiday one day in 1941 they found a Jewish family in their house (they had been allowed in by a friend) and they decided to let them stay while they and their three children went into furnished rooms. In August 1942 a former student asked if they could help 400 young Jews preparing to go to Palestine. They then recruited family members, friends and colleagues to help. Joop led between 300 and 400 of the group across Europe to Spain from where they hoped to reach Palestine. In December 1943 Will was arrested trying to bribe an internment guard. Three months later Joop was captured. He was tortured for 5 months and died without revealing a name or activity. Will survived the war.

Most rescue networks were informal and many did not have names. The Utrecht Children's Rescue Operation was a name given after the war. In 1940 Hetty Dutihl Voute was at the University of Amsterdam studying biology when two of her brothers started an underground newspaper and she became involved in its distribution. However her oldest brother was imprisoned and five out of seven of the family were eventually imprisoned for anti-Nazi activities. As the meaning of 'resettlement' dawned, Jewish children needed to be sheltered and Hetty along with a dozen or so friends began to organise rescue. She found a supplier of ration cards in southern Holland and went there monthly to pick them up. Money was raised including from the Archbishop of Utrecht and by selling 10,000 copies of a poem. They helped about 300 children but did not get to know them personally and used code names which were recorded in a book kept in Hetty's bookshelf. In June 1943 Hetty and colleague Gisela Wieberdink were returning from visiting a couple they were not sure of when they were arrested and sent to Ravensbruck. But the operation continued and when Hetty's book was located the Archbishop of Utrecht took responsibility for it. Later, British pilots were hidden too.

John Weidner, a Seventh-Day Adventist, was head of the Dutch-Paris underground network involving 300 resisters. Weidner himself used 11 different aliases. The network received finance from the World Council of Churches. 800 Jews and 100 Allied airmen were helped to cross the borders into Switzerland and Spain. Unfortunately one careless member had her list of contacts taken and half of the network were arrested. Forty were killed including Weidner's sister Gabrielle. Anje Roos was a young nurse who when the occupiers banned Jews from working in the hospital organised a petition protesting at this and all the patients signed it. In the spring of 1941 she rented a room in Amsterdam with three other nurses. Her roommates had many Jewish friends and on Fridays it became their custom to buy goods for them which Jews could not buy. Anje began work for a Jewish family as a baby nurse and one day the Gestapo called. She convincingly informed them that they had already been arrested for deportation. She then quickly arranged for them to move to another home in Utrecht. Later they were arrested when they unwisely took a walk in town. When Jewish friends asked her to help the Palestine Pioneer movement she eagerly did so. Soon her work of delivering documents, food and money to those in hiding became a full time job and she gave up nursing. Her family became involved and she brought Jews to their house and then on to safe houses in northern Holland. One of her brothers, Kais, who was a policeman worked in the Jewish quarter and would find as many Jews as possible when a raid was scheduled and would take them to a safe place, sometimes to the Dutch police office itself. Anje Roos then joined another group called Arondius which did sabotage. In March 1943 some dressed up as police officers and got into the Nazi registration office and set it on fire to destroy records of Jews. However careless talk led to the arrest of some of them and thirteen, including a brother, were shot. Anje Roos was sentenced to a year's hard labour in Ravensbruck. When she was released she was in poor health but soon resumed activities this time as a courier for an underground newspaper.

Cornelia Ten Boom's family led a rescue operation. They took Jews into their own home and found homes for others, supplying food coupons for all. They had a secret hiding room with four permanent residents which acted as a temporary home for others. Cornelia checked out potential new homes and regularly visited those in hiding, organising medical care and occasional burials. The whole family was involved but they were betrayed. The father died in prison and Cornelia and her sister and brother were sent to Ravensbruck where her sister and brother died also. Her staunch Christian faith helped her survive.

A businessman, Aart Vos, first became aware of how cruel the Nazis were when before the war he visited a family he knew in Germany and discovered one of the sons belonged to an organisation – later the Hitler Youth – which captured animals and killed them to condition the youths to accept violence as normal. When two Jewish musician friends had to move to the ghetto Aart and his wife Johtje agreed to look after their valuable grand piano and added that they would take their three-year-old son also. They lived in a two-story home in Laren and here they dug a tunnel from the house to a nature reserve a few hundred yards away. Here they sheltered three dozen Jews throughout the war. On one occasion when the Gestapo arrived Aart and the Jews hurried to the tunnel but Johtje had no time to hide incriminating documents so stuffed them into her son's jumper and told him to get out and hide. The raid passed over without discovery but Johtje was shocked when she realised the danger she had put her son in. On another occasion Aart Vos found a wounded soldier on the road and put him on his bicycle and took him to medical help, something which he was criticised for by a friend who saw all Germans as enemies. Johtje Vos's mother came one day not long after they had started hiding Jews and argued that she had no right as a mother to put her life at risk. Johtje later described how she and her husband saw things: "We find it more important for our children to have parents who have done what they felt they had to do – even if it costs their lives. It will be better for them – even if we don't make it. They will know we did what we felt we had to do. This is better than if we first think of our safety." The grandmother understood.

Fogelman, Eva, *Conscience and Courage: Rescuers of Jews During the Holocaust,* Anchor Books 1995

FATHER BRUNO AND BELGIAN RESCUERS

Father Bruno (Henry Reynders) was a scholarly Benedictine monk who rescued 320 Jewish children. His sympathy for the persecuted Jews was particularly aroused by something he had seen in Germany in 1938 – an elderly Jew dressed in a caftan and an old black hat was either being avoided by passers by or pointed at and sneared at; this deeply upset him.

As an army chaplain he was wounded in 1940 and was a prisoner of war for a year. On release he was sent by his Order to a home for the Blind which he discovered was largely a front for hiding Jews, although there were a few blind children, who were also Jewish. After a period the home became dangerous as too many people knew that Jews were being hidden there and so along with a lawyer from Liège, Albert Van den Berg, who was already involved in rescue, they had found by January 1943 ten families willing to shelter Jews. Van den Berg used his own money for the various needs of the children and Father Bruno received donations from relatives and friends for that purpose. After some months 159 adults and children had been placed in hiding but then his abbey office was raided by the Gestapo; fortunately he managed to hide incriminating material including the non-Jewish names that were being used by the children. He moved to Louvain and then Brussels to continue the work, where he lived next door to an SS captain of the Office of Jewish Affairs. Children and adults, including the Grand Rabbi of Liège, were placed in many religious institutions as well as private homes. The Rabbi survived the war but his parents were caught and deported to their deaths. Albert Van den Berg was arrested in April 1943 and died in Neuengamme concentration camp on the eve of liberation. Fr Bruno's last act was to place three children, age 8-10, with the Daughters of Charity in Asse, 8 miles from Brussels, before returning on foot to the city in time to see the German troops depart. Shortly after liberation Fr Bruno visited the Dutch synagogue in Brussels to say farewell to many of the children and the rabbi halted the service to announce his presence which was met with tumultuous applause.

Another clergyman, Abbot Joseph André, housed Jewish children in his monastery in Namur and in other nunneries and monasteries nearby. He also persuaded local families to hide Jews in their homes. He himself slept on the floor so that a Jew could have his bed. He carried food to families and messages from parents to their children; all the more remarkable as this was done from his home which was next to the hotel used by the Gestapo as their HQ. For the last few months of the war he had to go into hiding. More than 200 Jews were saved by his actions. After liberation Fr André made sure that the children who were orphaned were found homes with Jewish couples.

Yvonne Nèvejean, director of the National Agency for Children, played a major role in finding safe places for as many as 4,500 children. In addition to private homes, boarding schools, orphanages and convents were used. One of the children was five-year-old Bronia Veitch who had been born in Berlin. She was in a Jewish children's home when it was raided by the Gestapo on 30 October 1942 and 56 children and staff were taken to a camp. But the train was delayed and during this time the home's housekeeper phoned Nèvejean who contacted the Belgian Queen Mother Elisabeth who in turn intervened with the German High Command. A large ransom was also paid by the CDJ and the children were released. Other children on the train which eventually departed were all killed in Auschwitz-Birkenau. Bronia was placed with Henri and Gabrielle Bal who proved to be wonderful foster parents who managed to keep her safe until liberation. When the deportation of Jews with Belgium nationality began in mid-1943 the Bals paid the expenses of the Litvin family who went into hiding in Brussels.

The act of an SS officer was the almost miraculous saving of three-year-old Susan Preisz and her mother. They had been taken along with a crowd of terrified Jews to the Gestapo headquarters in Brussels. An SS officer asked who the child belonged to and the mother lifted Susan and managed to utter, "To me". The officer ordered her to follow him and then obtained a pail and water and a brush and told her to wash the stairs leading out of the cellar. After this was done the SS officer ordered her out of the building. Holding her daughter in her arms she walked home. Susan and her mother managed to survive the war in the countryside helped by non-Jews. One can only speculate as to what made the German officer act as he did.

A very similar instance concerned five-year-old Gisele Reich who in 1931 was at Malines awaiting deportation with her parents. Her father was deported first while Gisele waited with her mother. The child had poor health and this seemed to prompt a German officer to take pity on her and he asked her mother if she knew anyone who would look after Gisele. Her mother mentioned the Van de Velde family who were neighbours so the officer phoned them and they agreed to take her. They came immediately to collect Gisele and she stayed with them and their large family until she married.

A case of a civil servant resister was Léon Plateau, General Secretary of the Ministry of Justice, who used his position to obtain from the Germans the release of Jews from Dossin detention camp at Malines by annulment of the deportation orders to Auschwitz. He also transferred money to the Comité de Défense des Juifs (CDJ) every month sufficient to support 2,000 people long term.

A small village near Liège, Cornemont-Louveigné, with only ten families each took at least one Jewish child in spite of being searched frequently, the area being a centre of resistance.

Gilbert, Martin, *The Righteous: The Unsung Heroes of the Holocaust,* Black Swan 2002

Agnes Grunwald-Spier, *The Other Schindlers,* The History Press 2010

THE MODEL OCCUPATION

The Channel Islands – principally Jersey, Guernsey and Alderney – were the only part of the British Isles to be occupied by the Germans. Lying close to the Cotentin peninsula of the French mainland with a population of around 100,000 the British Government decided not to defend them and all military personnel and equipment were removed between 16 and 20 June 1940. This was followed by the evacuation of 30,000 islanders to the mainland. Unfortunately the Germans were not informed of the demilitarisation and so the Islands were bombed on 28 June resulting in 44 deaths. This was swiftly followed by the German occupation of the Islands.

Hitler decided that this would be a model occupation with as little conflict as possible and this suited the Islands' rulers too. The administration would continue as before except that laws had to be approved by the German commandant. Ambrose Sherwill, the Attorney General, was allowed to broadcast to Britain and, wishing to reassure relatives of Islanders, he painted such a rosy picture that it was a propaganda coup for the Germans.

But many changes were to follow for the islanders. Trade with Britain was cut off, and soon the Germans required labour for the airports which were being used in the Battle of Britain. The majority of the Islands' population were eventually working directly or indirectly for the Germans. All public organisations were brought under German control including the schools, libraries and the press and German language replaced French in the schools. The worst aspect of the occupation was the increasing shortage of food and fuel as the war progressed but this was eased at the end of 1944 when a Red Cross ship arrived with supplies. Nevertheless the death rate increased substantially due to malnutrition and the shortage of medicines.

Although the privations sometimes brought out the best in people such as sharing things in short supply there was a great increase in theft, including stealing from the Germans which was however considered by most as legitimate. Some people became informers. Violent resistance was almost impossible due to the high proportion of Germans and the absence of means of escape. But there was some nonviolent resistance by individuals, and sometimes it was coordinated. There were three occasions when demonstrations occurred. In September 1942 more than 2,000 Islanders were deported to camps in Germany on the orders of Hitler in retaliation for a British action; Islanders gathered on the quayside and sang 'Rule Britannia' and the National Anthem. Fortunately the conditions in the German camp proved to be relatively good. In June 1943 the bodies of two RAF men were washed ashore on Jersey. The Germans organised the funeral but thousands of Islanders attended and over 200 wreaths were laid. In October that year a British cruiser was sunk close to the Islands and the bodies of 21 sailors were washed up on Jersey. On 17 November the sailors were buried with full naval honours performed by the Germans. 4,000 Islanders attended and laid more than 400 wreaths. The Germans decided that future funerals would be quieter affairs.

In the summer of 1941 the BBC started the 'V for Victory' campaign. On the Islands V was chalked, by children as well as adults, on doors, walls and gateposts. Two young women stuck up cutout V signs near where Germans bathed, and being spotted, they were caught and sentenced to seven months in Caen prison. In June 1942 all radios were confiscated, a move that was extremely unpopular. In a few cases discovery of hidden radios led to deportation to Germany and not everyone survived to return. A cinema projectionist, Stanley Green, who hid his radio in the roof of the cinema was sent to Paris where he was tortured and then sent to Buchenwald, then to Munich where he was caught up in a bombing raid; he did survive but was only five stone in weight at the end and never fully recovered good health, although he lived to over 70. Uniquely he had been able to take photographs inside Buchenwald concentration camp which were used at the Nuremburg Trials.

Another familiar form of resistance developed on Guernsey too – an underground press. Journalist Charles Machon produced a daily news sheet from May 1942 to February 1944 but an informer who was an Irish citizen gave him away as well as four others. They were sent to the continent where Machon and one other died. On Jersey the Bulletin of British Patriots was produced by two brothers, Herbert and George Gallichan. It called on people not to give up their radios and it tried to expose collaborators. The Germans took ten hostages in June 1944 until the group surrendered. George Gallichan was imprisoned in Dijon and his brother in Wolfenbuttel camp until the end of the war.

Two wealthy French sisters, Lucille Schwab and Suzanne Malherbe,, tried to incite mutiny on Jersey by putting typed notes attacking Hitler and Germany in public places and slipping them into the coat pockets of Germans. They were artists who had associated with the surrealists in Paris and then retired to Jersey where they had spent childhood holidays. They were arrested in July 1944 and held in solitary confinement for six months. Germans searching their house found paintings by Picasso and Miro and others, which were apparently destroyed. The sisters were sentenced to death in 1945 but after a plea from the Bailiff of Jersey this was commuted to life imprisonment and they were released on liberation.

An unusual gesture of personal resistance was by Mrs Winifred Green of Guernsey who was sent to prison for uttering 'Heil Churchill' while working as a waitress at the Royal Hotel; after 4 months in Caen she was released and returned to her job.

The darkest aspect of the occupation concerned the 16,000 foreign workers who were brought to the Islands to work on constructing massive fortifications as Hitler thought that Britain might try to retake the Islands. The workers were brought by the Todt Organisation which used a mixture of volunteers and forced workers. About half were effectively slaves and most of them came from eastern Europe. For these slave workers conditions were atrocious with starvation level food and a working day of 12 hours. The smallest of the three islands, Alderney, had the worst conditions and brutality by the guards was routine.

On Guernsey a Salvation Army member, Marie Ozanne, protested about the treatment of the workers and was arrested and imprisoned. She died a few months after being released in 1943. On Jersey there was a network of families who hid escaped slave workers. There were at least 20 escapees in hiding on liberation; some had been hidden for nearly two years. Bob Le Suer helped to find hiding places but his own home was too close to a German blockhouse to be safe. He became friendly with a Russian, Feodor Burryiy (known as Bill), who had tried to escape but was caught and punished by being put in a freezing bath and left naked outside overnight. A few days later he escaped again and was hidden by a farmer with five children who was already hiding two other Russians. Bob Le Suer then found found a widow, Louise Gould, who had just lost her son while serving in the navy, who was willing to take Bill in.

Her sister Ivy Fisher also sheltered a Russian. Bill, being in danger of discovery, was then taken to two conscientious objectors who had come to Jersey in 1940. When Louise's house was searched in June 1944 the Germans found some paper on which Bill had been practising English so she was arrested and sent to prison on the continent. She died in Ravensbruck aged 53. Ivy was also given a prison sentence, on the island, for having a radio. Louise's brother, Harold Le Druillenec, was arrested also for having a radio and ended up in Belsen but in spite of the appalling conditions did survive. 'Bill' remained in hiding till Liberation.

Albert Bedane, a physiotherapist living in St Helier, Jersey, had a secret cellar under his clinic which was attached to his house. In it he sheltered several escaped Russian prisoners and also a Jewish woman, Mary Richardson, who was Dutch-born married to a British sea captain. She lived there for two-and-a-half years until liberation.

A woman who was married to an hotelier was generally assumed to be pro-German since she was an Austrian national and in addition Germans had taken over the hotel for recreation. But in fact she was anti-Nazi and her father and brother were Social Democrats who were sent to Mauthausen. She hid two Russians in the attic for two years feeding them scraps from the hotel kitchen.

Stella Perkins lived in a flat in the centre of St Helier. Her mother and aunt were Russians who had met Stella's father when he was a member of the expedition sent to Archangel in 1914 to defeat the Bolsheviks. He returned with them to England, later moving to Jersey. Stella's flat became a meeting place for escaped Russians, some staying for months. The older women enjoyed the company of those who spoke their native language.

The last year of the war was increasingly difficult as supplies became used up without being replaced. Churchill would not authorise supplies as he wanted the Germans to surrender. Eventually supplies were authorised and in spite of the Germans being as short of food as the Islanders the latter did receive them.

There was a very small number of Communists on the Islands including Norman Le Brocq who produced news bulletins in French, Spanish and Russian which were distributed in the slave labourers' camps. After the liberation of France a German soldier and socialist, Paul Mulbach, made contact with the Communists to plan a mutiny but before they were able to strike, the Islands were surrendered by the Germans on 9 May 1945.

From the beginning of the occupation the Islands' administrators had decided that compromise and collaboration made sense. This suited the Germans also who wanted as little conflict as possible. On the whole Jersey compromised less than Guernsey. Soon after the occupation the Guernsey Attorney General, Ambrose Sherwill, enacted legislation making "any behaviour by a civilian likely to cause a deterioration in the relations between the occupying forces and the civilian population" an offence. During the V-sign campaign the Guernsey police handed over to the Germans Islanders who had been caught writing V-signs. The Guernsey Bailiff, Victor Carey, offered rewards to islanders to inform on those writing V-signs. When the 2,000 Islanders were deported it was the local administration that drew up the lists and organised the deportation. There were only around 20 Jews remaining on the island at occupation but nevertheless anti-Jewish legislation was introduced. Their fates varied: some survived on the Islands, some were deported and some of these survived while some perished. However relations between the majority of the islanders and the ordinary German soldiers were generally friendly and in the case of quite a few young women romances developed with members of the Wehrmacht, a few leading to marriages after the war.

Bunting, Madeleine, *The Model Occupation: The Channel Islands under German Rule 1940-45,* Harper Collins 1996

Responses to Occupation

THE OCCUPIERS

The German invaders, at first sight surprisingly, did not impose the same type of rule on all the countries they occupied. In fact there was very considerable variation. One influence was the view of the occupied populace held by the occupier. Nazi racist ideology led to a different attitude towards the people they considered Aryan, for example, Norwegians and Danes, compared with Slavs, that is Poles and Russians, who were considered racially inferior. Another influence was the composition of the invaded country, for example, whether a strong collaborationist faction existed, as in France. However even when there was considerable similarity, such as Norway and Denmark, sometimes other factors came into play: the Norwegians decided to resist while the Danes at first collaborated.

Some of the occupied territories were simply annexed to Germany, such as Western Poland and Gdansk, Silesia, and Luxemburg, Alsace and part of Lorraine.

A commoner form of governance was direct administration but using the local civil service such as in Belgium, the Netherlands, Norway, most of France, and the parts of Poland not annexed by Germany or Russia. In Norway, Joseph Terboven directed a Norwegian administration containing pro-Nazis; the Netherlands had a civil administration under the control of Dr Artur Seyss-Inquart with the Dutch Secretaries of State who were recognised by the Government-in-Exile; in Belgium the Secretaries General, senior civil servants, came under the control of General Falkenhausen; more than half of France was run by the German military; the parts of Poland not annexed by Germany or Russia were called the General Government which was headed by General Hans Frank.

Another form was guardianship which gave the appearance of local autonomy, such as the southern zone of France (Vichy, headed by Marshal Henri Pétain); the eastern part of Czechoslovakia (headed by Monsignor Josef Tiso); Denmark whose government remained in place until August 1943; and Yugoslavia which was run by local fascists. In general the indigenous fascist parties were sidelined by the Germans who preferred to use the more representative bodies who were nevertheless willing to collaborate with a powerful occupying force.

Finally there were the independent allies of Germany – Romania, Hungary, Bulgaria, Finland, and Italy, but the latter being occupied by Germany after the fall of Mussolini's government.

German forces did not just occupy territory but also used the occupied countries' resources of food and manufactures to strengthen Germany itself and in addition used the workforce through conscription for work in Germany itself. Using the resources of conquered territory was of enormous importance to the strength of the Reich and consequently the duration of the war.

COLLABORATION

The Dutch historian Louis de Jong has said, "almost everyone practised resistance and collaboration at one and the same time". [Rings p.128]

Fascist groups in the occupied countries were less favoured by the occupiers and less important to them than might have been expected. In Norway the Nasjonal Samling (National Unity Party) led by Vidkun Quisling had great hopes of governing the country but it ultimately failed. In western Europe the pro-Nazi parties were not chosen by the Germans for the major role that they hoped for. In the Netherlands the pro-Nazi party led by Anton Mussert had 100,000 members yet was not given a significant role. Mussert was unusual in that he was not anti-Semitic and shared with Quisling the idea of a strong independent country that would not be absorbed into the Reich. He banned members of the National Socialist Movement (NSB) from joining the SS but many members were recruited by the Germans to such roles as mayors and informers. Dr Fritz Clausen in Denmark was a model Nazi but the last general election in 1943 demonstrated how unpopular he and his party were and the occupiers dropped them. In Belgium the pro-Nazis were weakened by the old division between Walloon and Flemish culture which was deliberately reinforced by the Germans who were not interested in bringing them to power. In France the two leading collaborators came from the political left. Jacques Doriot was a metalworker and leading Communist who was expelled from the Communist Party and adopted fascism. Marcel Déat was a professor of philosophy and a member of the Socialist Party and a deputy. He was expelled from the Socialist Party along with other deputies and his thought moved in an authoritarian direction. Both men founded new parties but Hitler made limited use of them.

Cooperation with less ideologically committed people who were prepared on pragmatic grounds to cooperate with the occupier was the favoured route of the Nazis. This included the civil servants or those in essential services such as transport and electricity supplies. France was a special case where Marshall Pétain and the Vichy Government mixed pragmatism with some shared ideology with the occupiers. The principal aim of the collaboration in this case was to preserve what they understood as French culture as well as a French state which would acquire full status again in the future. But for the long term survival of an occupying regime legitimacy needs to be established in the eyes of the majority population of the occupied and Vichy went some way to supplying that for the Germans.

As Germany plundered the occupied territories it became a major activity of the occupied population to find food and other essentials and thus resistance was not a top priority for most people – day-to-day survival took up people's energies. However, dissent began to appear and increased with time. People listened to radio programmes coming from abroad; workers would often go-slow deliberately and would sometimes sabotage production by making mistakes or misinterpreting orders; officials would sometimes warn people of imminent raids by the police; symbols of resistance would be worn on clothes; underground papers would be produced and distributed. Some people worked normally during the day but undertook resistance work at night.

As time passed it became more difficult to combine cooperation with resistance. In Belgium the heads of the administrative departments stayed in post but it became increasingly difficult for them to carry out distasteful German orders, for example actions against Jews. In Denmark cooperation led in time to increasing conflict which eventually culminated in the Germans taking direct control.

The situation in Poland and certain other eastern territories differed from western Europe as the Germans did not seek collaboration at all but simply used repression. (Contrary to Hitler's desire, however, the Wehrmacht enlisted Cossacks and others in the east due to a shortage of fighting men.) A disadvantage to the occupier of using repression was that the population responded with widespread resentment and intensified opposition. As a consequence the Poles in time developed almost an alternative clandestine state. With regard to the Jews, the Germans used Jewish Councils (Judenrät) to smooth the way for deportation and extermination. Similar Councils existed in some other occupied countries.

The occupiers required cooperation from the administrations and railroad and electrical services of the occupied as they did not have sufficient personpower to to keep them functioning themselves. This was in fact usually available to them. In Belgium the railroad and electrical employees had actually received a Civilian Mobilisation Handbook in 1937 calling on them not to offer resistance in the event of a foreign invasion but to carry on working normally. In the Netherlands civil servants had envelopes to be opened in the event of invasion giving procedures to be followed and these were similar to Belgium's. In Belgium and Holland the civil servants mostly agreed to work with the occupying administration for the sake of the general population. Some administrators in Belgium decided to stay in place to soften the impact of the occupation by using as a pretext the unconstitutionality of undesirable proposals of the occupiers. The heads of departments, called General Secretaries, ended up acting like Ministers forming a 'college'. Many Judges also remained in place although a few fled abroad. In practice it was not a successful tactic, for example, the October 1940 anti-Jewish orders were administered by the provincial governors. In late 1942 the lawyers went on strike and some arrests were made but the strike did not last long and the outcome was more concessions.

In France most of the industrial centres were occupied and the French had to pay for the upkeep of the German army of occupation. France also became Germany's main food source. The occupiers had economic and administrative support from the French. In the south the Pétain regime collaborated with the Germans and when Admiral Darlan joined the administration in February 1941 military collaboration increased. When Pierre Laval, who was strongly pro-German, became Prime Minister in April 1942 relations with the Germans became closer still. The Vichy regime was more strongly anti-socialist than anti-German. After the German take-over of the south in November 1942 many French workers were dispatched to Germany and Jews were more actively sought out. In employment, collaboration was widespread. Private businesses as well as individuals were often willing to collaborate with German businesses and the government. Millions of European workers voluntarily migrated to Germany to work in the armaments industry in the first two years of the war. 59,000 French workers took jobs in Germany in the first 16 months of the occupation; in spring 1942, 845,000 French workers were employed exclusively on behalf of the Third Reich. By the end of 1942 German contracts with France were for 3,620 aircraft and 11,780 aero engines. 403,000 Belgians worked for the Germans; 82,000 were employed by the Todt organisation to construct fortifications and airfields in Belgium; about 80% of coal mined was for Germany. In Denmark 103,000 workers in the first 14 months of occupation went to Germany to work in spite of attempts by the trade unions to dissuade them. Denmark even exported more foodstuffs than were required by the quota agreement. In Poland, by May 1940, 210,000 Poles had gone to work in Germany. In the USSR one million people worked for the occupiers. Throughout Europe, industrialists, financiers and businessmen placed factories and financial services too at the Third Reich's disposal.

Dutch railway workers collaborated with the Germans and this included dispatching 98 trains carrying 112,000 Dutch Jews to the extermination camps. When late in the war the railway workers changed sides and on 17 September 1944 struck in support of the Arnhem landings they demanded full pay, plus overtime, for the duration of the strike and were given it. This cost 44% of all the financial aid received by the Dutch Resistance.

Mayors and police were often used by the Germans in anti-Jewish measures. (Polish police forces were the least involved.) In France, the Milice, the Parti Populaire Francais and others of the political right helped in round-ups of Jews and also in their murder. In the more anti-Semitic countries such as Latvia, Lithuania, Poland, Romania and Hungary the Germans could rely on a minority of the population to betray Jews or actively persecute them independently.

Many physicians in Germany even welcomed the expulsion of Jewish doctors as it eliminated the professional competition, and similarly the lawyers. By 1938 Jewish doctors and lawyers were restricted to Jewish patients and clients.

An unexpected collaboration occurred by some Red Army units led by General Andrei Vlasov, a distinguished general and member of the Communist Party since 1930. After successful battles, in the spring of 1942 his army was surrounded in the Volkhov area and he was captured and taken to the German headquarters in the Ukraine. Here he met another Red Army officer and a Political Commissar and after discussions they found they held similar views: anti-Stalin and anti-dictatorship. They would have preferred to seek help from the Western Powers but that was not possible so they proposed a collaboration to rid Russia of Stalinism but on condition that Russia was not occupied by the Germans. Without informing Hitler the German generals accepted the offer and an army was formed from Russian prisoners. However Hitler heard of this and Vlasov was never given permission to fight the Red Army although the Germans used him for propaganda purposes. When Vlasov was moved to a villa in Berlin the recruited Russians began to desert although some were, ironically, sent to fight on the Western Front against the democracies. In the last days of the war Vlasov marched a force of nearly 100,000 into American prison camps but they were later handed over to the Russians and Vlasov and other senior officers were executed.

ACCOMMODATION

Adapting to a totally new situation was difficult and time was needed to develop new patterns of behaviour and new institutions. Self-preservation became the overwhelming aim. The occupied countries were plundered by Germany and thus the people had to spend much time and energy searching for food and other essentials Some accommodation was essential for survival. Probably the majority of the occupied populace remained in that state.

Denmark was less severely dealt with than any other occupied country and retained considerable self-governance yet the Government compromised by expressing the wish to build a Germanic Europe and it broke off relations with the USA and USSR and joined the anti-Commintern Pact. It also outlawed the Communist Party and imprisoned communists which was against the constitution, as well as agreeing to the establishment of a Danish Free Corps to fight on the eastern front. But collaboration was more clearly than elsewhere a two-way arrangement that for a time suited both parties.

RESISTANCE

Dissent developed slowly: people listened to radio broadcasts from abroad; some would collaborate during the day in their work and then resist at night. Officials could sometimes warn people of imminent arrests or raids. The business community usually collaborated with the occupiers so workers used slowdowns and technical sabotage such as removal of essential pieces of equipment so that the quality of the goods was reduced. Misinterpreting orders also reduced efficiency.

Nevertheless the combination of accommodation with resistance became difficult to maintain. In Denmark it came to a head in August 1943 when growing dissatisfaction led to conflict and a different relationship. In Belgium, the heads of administrative departments stayed in post but increasingly had to carry out directives they did not agree with.

Repression by the occupier increased from a relatively low level dealing with demonstrations, to a greater level with strikes, then with violent sabotage, to assassinations with the latter being met with the most fierce repression. However even distributing anti-government leaflets could lead to imprisonment and execution. Potential resistance groups included clergy, doctors, teachers, civil servants, police, political parties, students, actors, musicians, sportspeople, trade unionists in railways, docks, factories, construction. Different groups were more active or effective in different countries. Factors which aided resistance were countries with a democratic tradition, which in addition had a high urban concentration, and the resisters had a high social cohesion supported by public opinion. If they did not resort to arms they had greater protection from violent attacks. However insufficient coordination of the resistance groups may have been a weak aspect of the resistance.

Producing clandestine newspapers was among the commonest and most important forms of resistance. Holland and Poland both had about 1,200, France 1,034, Norway and Denmark 852, Belgium 500. *Defence de La Resistance* reached a peak of 450,000 copies. A Dutch resistance newspaper, *Trouw*, had a circulation of 60,000. The Germans found it difficult to extinguish *Trouw* and in summer 1944 they made an offer of releasing from prison those linked to the paper who had been caught in return for closure of the paper. The offer was refused and 23 of these prisoners were executed. *Trouw* lost a total of 120 associates to firing squads yet the circulation of all newspapers in January 1945 was about 2 million.

The authorities were put in a dilemma by the use of nonviolent forms of action. German generals who were interrogated after the war admitted they often did not know how to deal with nonviolent actions. In contrast, assassinations, and other violent acts by the resisters met with counter violence, sometimes extreme as in the case of the killing of Reinhard Heydrich by a small number of Czechs which resulted in retaliation that included the obliteration of the village of Lidice; also the killing of 98 French hostages for the assassination of one German officer in Nantes. Repression did not work well for the Germans in Poland especially because it was indiscriminate and so there was no advantage in conforming; minor infringements of the law were treated as severely as major ones.

Financial support either internally or from abroad was of great importance to the organised resistance. In Poland teachers were paid by the Government in London. In Denmark skippers of boats used in the rescue of Jews were paid by the general public. In Belgium the Jewish Defence Committee received funds from American Jews operating through Switzerland. Teachers in Norway were supported financially by parents. In Holland a National Fund for Mutual Aid was set up to bring assistance to many different groups; loans were guaranteed by the Government-in-Exile which employed thousands of people.

The nature of the population occupied was a factor of significance. Norway and Denmark were relatively homogeneous ethnically and religiously which resulted in a certain cohesion which was an advantage in resistance. Another factor was traditional attitudes to Jews, whether they were seen as integral to the society or in some way alien. An important external factor was nearness to a neutral country such as Sweden or Switzerland so that escape across the border was a possibility. By the end of 1943 Switzerland had 64,000 refugees including 10,000 Jews. Sweden had 53,000 refugees including 11,000 Jews.

Probably a greater difficulty for resisters than violent suppression was the insidious economic strain such as threats of loss of jobs, shortage of food, fuel and other essentials.

Beyond the Nazi Sphere
of Influence

Resistance and rescue within the occupied territories was influenced not just by policies and actions of the Reich representatives nor externally by the armed forces of the Allies but by actions and policies of states outside the occupied territory that did not involve overt violence.

The existence of countries not involved in the war, especially those with a common frontier with the greater Reich played an important role throughout the war. The neutral countries of Sweden, Switzerland and Spain provided a relatively safe destination for those sought by the Nazis.

Many organisations came into being to provide escape routes for those endangered. Switzerland took in 28,000 people from France but over 12,000 of these had entered clandestinely and well over a thousand were turned away to almost certain capture. It was the individual cantons which decided who to admit in most instances. Although 26,000 Jews were admitted nearly as many were refused. Switzerland was dependent on trade for about half of its food and nearly all its fuel so it dealt with other countries including Germany. Both Germans and the Allies sold gold to the Swiss National Bank. The Reichsbank sold large quantities of gold in exchange for foreign currency.

Although Sweden was an important destination for refugees from Norway and most of the Danish Jews survived because they were allowed in, the transport of German troops through Sweden was controversial. Over one million German troops passed through Sweden to Norway or Finland although they were mostly unarmed troops going on leave to Germany or wounded. An exception was one division of combat-ready troops going to Finland. Both types of movement violated neutrality.

A more distant destination for refugees was Shanghai. Frank Foley, British passport control officer in Berlin (and also an MI6 officer), provided documents for Jews to travel to Shanghai, as well as the more conventional destinations of Britain and Palestine, where the Japanese refused to hand them over to the Nazis. There had been a community of Jews in Shanghai since 1842 and it was the only city in the world where refugees did not require a visa to enter. Foley's work only lasted until war was declared as he was then recalled home but he had been able to help thousands of Jews escape from Germany.

Money was very important to the various underground organisations within the occupied territories and clandestine routes were found to get it to where it was needed. The governments-in-exile often supplied large sums to their nationals in the undergrounds and in the case of the Jews American Jewish funds were very important.

The possibility of escape from Nazi territory for dissidents and Jews was limited by the willingness of the free countries to provide access. This was often something which the governments did reluctantly and there were strict controls on the numbers of immigrants. The Jewish community in Britain paid for the resettlement of German Jews. The Kindertransport or escape of Jewish children from the continent to Britain just before war broke out was one that was allowed by the British Government. Nicholas Winton, a young stockbroker, had been introduced to the plight of children in Prague by an academic, Doreen Warriner, of the British Committee for Refugees from Czechoslovakia. Some four million pounds was provided by the British Government for the resettlement of refugees in Czechoslovakia or abroad but not in Britain itself. Winton drew up a list of those in danger and when he returned to London began to look for sponsors and families who would take the children. In total 669 children reached Britain from Prague before the outbreak of war brought the rescue to an end. There were Kindertransports from Germany and Austria also totalling nearly 10,000 children and many organisations were formed to help.

In the pre-war period the number of refugees from Germany and Austria, predominantly Jewish, admitted to various countries was: to USA 57,000, to France 40,000, to Belgium 25,000, to Switzerland 10,000, to Britain 65,000 and to Palestine 53,000. Jewish immigration to Palestine from wider Europe was 215,000 and this more than doubled the Jewish population there.

On the outbreak of war British immigration rules were made even more stringent. For security reasons immigration from enemy territory was almost prohibited, although a small number were allowed in during 1940 from the Netherlands, Belgium and France. The Government claimed that in the period 1940-42, 63,000 refugees had been admitted to Britain, but in fact most of these were Allied nationals or those useful for the war effort. Early in 1943 the Home Secretary, Herbert Morrison, said that up to 2,000 refugees would be accepted if the Dominions and the USA accepted a proportionate number. He noted that 100,000 refugees, mostly Jews, were already in Britain and this had to be viewed in the light of extensive destruction of housing which had taken place during the blitz of 1940-41. The British government was also concerned about large numbers of refugee Jews which might lead to growing anti-Semitism and the British Jews were aware of that themselves. Some refugees arriving in Britain moved on to other countries.

Britain also kept strict control of immigration to Palestine. 12,000 per year was the limit in the 1930s and then a ceiling of 75,000 operated till 31 March 1944 with no further Jews allowed in without the consent of the Arabs. But when war began a ban on immigration from Nazi-occupied territory was introduced to prevent Nazi agents slipping in and so the overall ceiling was not reached. This was a great disappointment to the British Jews.

Immigration restrictions to the USA were determined by the quotas which they had for immigrants based on country of origin. Germany, Britain and the USA all gave consideration to settling Jews in various other countries, the most frequently mentioned being Madagascar but there were others in Africa and Latin America and even Alaska.

Jews in eastern Europe had even worse prospects for while expulsion from German territories was the initial aim of the Nazis this soon turned into murder by the Einsatzgruppen squads on the order of Hitler.

During the war the overriding aim was defeat of the Axis forces and everything including the plight of the continental Jews was subordinate to that. The failure of the Allied air forces to bomb the gas chambers at Auschwitz is indicative of that.

Another influence from outside the Nazi zone was the radio broadcast, particularly that of the BBC. Programmes were broadcast in 47 languages and were listened to on hidden radios for those fortunate to have access and were a very important source of news which the underground press disseminated. General de Gaulle often used it too to encourage resistance. In 1942 General Sikorski, head of the Polish Government-in- Exile, broadcast to Poland to condemn the murder of Polish Jews, and a member of the Jewish Socialist Bund, Szmul Zygielbojm, sent a message in Yiddish. The Archbishop of Westminster, Cardinal Hinsley, broadcast a message aimed at Catholics condemning the persecution of Jews. A broadcast to Belgium in December 1942 encouraged the hiding of Jews by Belgian citizens and the Dutch Prime Minister, Professor Gerbrandy, denounced the deportation of Dutch Jews. The Czechoslovak Foreign Minister, Jan Masaryk, made a powerful appeal for his countrymen and women to help the Jews whenever they could. The BBC also in October 1943 issued a warning to Jews sixteen times in eleven languages and appealed to non-Jews to give Jews shelter. The Archbishop of Canterbury in mid-1944 broadcast to

Hungarian Christians appealing for them to do their utmost to help Jews even at risk to themselves. However the total broadcast time given to the Jewish plight was not large.

FACTORS FOR SUCCESS

According to Semelin a united front by the occupied populace to the invader would be most likely to achieve success. Thus a more homogeneous population may have an advantage and one can see that in the cases of Norway and Denmark which had considerable ethnic and religious homogeneity. On the other hand Belgium displayed strong resistance in spite of the two communities of French speaking Walloons and the Flemish speaking Flemish community.

Countries with strong democratic traditions and active grass roots societies were perhaps more likely to establish non-cooperation with the intruder, such as the Netherlands, Belgium, Norway, and Denmark where professional unions resisted Nazification.

A tradition of tolerance and near absence of anti-Semitism gave some protection to minorities, such as in Italy, Denmark and Bulgaria.

The availability of food is essential and rural economies probably have an advantage here. But in the Netherlands in the last year of the war the Germans prevented food from getting into the cities which caused famine.

The availability of money is another essential, and particularly difficult for those living underground, and here governments-in-exile and other organisations outside the country were able to transfer it across national boundaries.

Nonviolent action can create or intensify divisions among the occupiers, such as in Denmark between the Reich Commissar and the Wehrmacht, or in Norway between rivals Terboven and Quisling.

Actions which did not succeed in their immediate aim could nevertheless have longer term effects. The widespread Dutch strike of 1943 led to immediate repression but it did show that the populace could act collectively and this reduced their fear and submissiveness. The 1943 release of workers for deportation at Montluçon station was unsuccessful in that they were recaptured but knowledge of the action spread by underground newspapers and increased confidence in the possibility of resisting.

Although difficult to achieve, trying to distinguish between the occupier as a person and the occupier as a functionary thus leading to a friendly attitude in the first case is recommended by Johan Galtung, and was indeed practised by some individuals. This is very much a Gandhian approach.

The effect a particular mass nonviolent action – the 1941 Luxemburg strike – had on one German official is described by W Bosseler and R Streichen: "He had not foreseen such courage and such ferocious will to resist. He thought it possible that there might be still more revolts, and his personal interest and fear of dismissal made him try to avoid measures that were too general and too grand that could make the population of Luxemburg respond collectively."
[Semelin p.174]

Semelin came to the conclusion that the likelihood of success in a conflict is increased if it is collective, nonviolent and open.

A more recent large scale empirical study of nonviolent movements operating under severe conditions is by Erica Chenoweth and Maria Stephan. They have come up with some remarkable observations. They examined 323 campaigns around the world covering the years 1900 to 2006, one third of these used nonviolent methods and two thirds used violent methods,. These struggles were aimed at removing oppressive regimes or defeating invaders. The principal finding is that nonviolent campaigns are twice as often successful as those using violence.

The main reason for this success they believe is that nonviolent campaigns attract more participants. They found that the average nonviolent campaign had about 200,000 participants in contrast to only 50,000 for the violent campaigns. Remarkably, nonviolent movements were revealed to be as effective against violent-authoritarian regimes as they were against peaceful-democratic regimes. This seems to apply irrespective of geographical location and is also persistent over time. The authors quote a study by Eleanor Marchant and others who found that the success of nonviolent campaigns is very little affected by the type of regime, by its level of development, or whether it is a country divided along ethnic, religious or linguistic lines. This appears in part to be counter to Semelin's conclusions. Another aspect in favour of nonviolent campaigns is that they are more likely to lead to stable democratic regimes in the long term. Something not examined by the authors is the number of casualties resulting from the two types of campaign which is surely a relevant consideration also. Although there are nonviolent campaigns that fail and violent campaigns that succeed this wide-ranging study reveals a clear statistical advantage for the superiority of pragmatic nonviolent action.

THE COSTS OF WAR

In war the antagonists focus primarily on the end to be achieved – defeating the enemy. The means to that end follow next, and only last the cost of reaching the desired end. But the cost of war can be enormous. In the Second World War, leaving aside the Asian sphere and looking only at the European conflict, it resulted in approximately 45 million deaths, two-thirds of which were of civilians. The injured probably amounted to several times the number of dead. Then there was the enormous destruction of houses and industrial buildings, schools and hospitals and cultural treasures; and the millions of refugees created.

Moral slippage is almost inevitable in war unless it ends quickly. Initially the aim of bombing populated areas was primarily to destroy militarily useful hardware and killing of civilians was an unintentional consequence. As a prelude to the D-Day landings massive bombing of rail junctions by the Allies led to many French civilian deaths and this was considered by the Allied Supreme Command as acceptable. Later, matters went a stage further with the deliberate killing of civilians with the aim of destroying the morale of the populace. This included mass bombing the cities of Hamburg, Dresden, Cologne and Berlin by the Allied air forces, often creating fire storms in which everything was consumed.

Another consequence of the massive struggle was that the official conclusion of the war did not end the killing because in the formerly occupied countries reprisals perpetrated by the local populations were widespread. Collaborators were singled out for humiliating and brutal treatment; shaving the heads of women who had fraternised with the occupiers and parading them in public is familiar but much worse treatment was sometimes meted out to Germans simply because they were German. German civilians were shot en masse or beaten to death, particularly in eastern Europe, others died of disease and starvation in the concentration camps which were now reoccupied by the former enemy. This treatment even included children. This behaviour was due to a coarsening of the moral sense which came with the intensification of the war as it progressed.

At the end of the war thousands of former Nazis, sometimes of the worst sort such as Klaus Barbie, were recruited by the Allies, particularly the Americans, as they were considered useful in combatting the new enemy – the Soviet Union. The extension of the Soviet empire itself was a consequence of the war so that another totalitarian state consolidated itself as one fell. As the 'hot war' cooled it was followed by decades of the Cold War with the new antagonists armed with a weapon of truly awesome destructive power which was itself developed as a direct consequence of the war.

Is it likely that a nonviolent defence, while costly against a fanatical opponent, would reach these levels of cruelty, killing and destruction ?

WHO WERE THE RESISTERS AND THE RESCUERS ?

Among resisters, as distinct from rescuers, those who held a strong ideology were prominent. This included strongly committed Communists as well as those with a very firm religious faith. The staunchest of all religious resisters were Jehovah's Witnesses who suffered greatly from their refusal to serve the oppressor. Those of other denominations were collectively much less united in opposition, but for some individuals their stance derived from deep religious faith. For others ardent patriotism was often a driving force.

The motivations of rescuers were studied by sociologists Samuel and Pearl Oliner (Samuel being a Polish rescued survivor) using a sample of 682 individuals of whom 406 were rescuers, 126 non-rescuers and 150 rescued survivors. There was a considerable degree of consistency in the findings.

There were several types of help that rescuers of Jews could give: they could help them in a variety of ways as the state persecution evolved over time; they could help them escape from places of incarceration; they could help them hide; they could help them escape to a safe country. Some rescuers carried out one of these tasks, often for different individuals; some performed as many as four. Valued possessions of Jews were often accepted by non-Jews for safe keeping. Rescuers who made up convincing stories and acted confidently could sometimes get Jews released. Germans on occasion would turn a blind eye. Bribing could be effective too in dealing with some individuals. Although a single rescuer working alone might provide a hiding place for one or more persons it was more common for networks to evolve and these sometimes consisted of hundreds of people, which did however make them vulnerable to being uncovered. Sheltering places included attics, cellars, sewers, ditches, pigsties, haystacks, closets, underground dugouts, and others.

The Oliners found that both rescuers and non-rescuers became aware of the way Jews were treated by the occupiers although they may not have known until fairly late in the war that Jews were actually being systematically exterminated. However non-rescuers were more likely to dismiss the stories as probably not true or they may not have grasped the significance of what they knew even when they personally observed discrimination or brutality. Risks varied in different places – for example, the populace was treated differently in different countries by the Germans – and at different times. Although money was important to the rescue process, the individual financial status of rescuers did not seem to matter. It was found that there was a wider range from wealthy to poor among the rescuers than among the non-rescuers who were mostly in the middle range. But more rescuers did have larger houses, which would have been advantageous for hiding others. Rescuers also had larger networks of sympathetic individuals who were likely to give support and this was important. As many as a third of rescuers initiated the approach to a needy person themselves, while the majority were asked for help by a friend who was an intermediary or sometimes directly by the person in need.

The Oliners believed that although chance sometimes brought rescuers the opportunity to help, the principles that led them to act were developed in childhood. The way in which children were brought up by their parents led the children to develop values that in adulthood made them potential rescuers. In these individuals disciplining in childhood was accompanied by explanations as to why they should act in a certain way rather than given on the parents' authority only. While most parents at that time were Christian, their understanding of Christianity could in reality differ and lead them to different attitudes to Jews or to Germans or to what one's responsibilities were. Those who grew up with a basic understanding of the equality of all people, all people being worthy of respect irrespective of religion or race, were more likely to act as rescuers. Another extremely important quality that rescuers displayed and the rescued recognised was care or compassion.

The Oliners described their main finding: "For most rescuers helping Jews was an expression of ethical principles that extended to all of humanity and, while often reflecting concern with equity and justice, was predominantly rooted in care." That this was an enduring characteristic of rescuers was demonstrated by the voluntary activities that former rescuers got involved with in their post-war lives.

Eva Fogelman, a social psychologist whose father had been saved by a Russian, also made a study of people who became rescuers. She was interested in the experiments of Stanley Milgram who found that individuals when instructed by experimenters to give electric shocks to a vulnerable subject (who was actually an actor) would do so even in some cases to very dangerous levels. Orders given by an authority figure were usually obeyed but she was more interested in the minority who disobeyed and refused to give the shocks. This led her to contact many rescuers of Jews, those who had not followed the majority, to interview them at length to seek their motivations. She found that she could identify five distinct groups:

1. Those whose conscience led them to act whether from religious motives such as holding firmly to the teachings of their church or faith or philosophical beliefs.
2. Those with a political ideology opposed to Nazism; these were often members of networks of resisters. Fogelman found this group to be very largely from business or professional families.
3. Those who were Judeophilic – people who felt a special relationship to an individual Jew or to Jewish people as a group.

4. Another was people like doctors, nurses, teachers and social workers whose occupations involved helping others; they had a more detached professional outlook.
5. Children who helped Jews because their parents did so.

Usually people became rescuers when they were asked by friends or acquaintances if they could help. The ability to help, however, depended not just on willingness but on the availability of a hiding place which was reasonably secure and the ability to get extra food. In addition, to avoid discovery rescuers had to be able to act normally in stressful situations, a characteristic that by no means everyone possessed. Generally the humanitarian outlook of the rescuers was retained throughout their lives – it was a consistent part of their character. During the war rescuers would sometimes help individual German soldiers who were in distress as they were able to see beyond the uniform to the vulnerable person. One special group that had the means to help on a large scale were diplomats as they were able to produce documents which could aid the victims and they were also less exposed to serious consequences, although danger was not totally absent.

Fogelman found certain characteristics in the family background of many of the rescuers: a nurturing, loving home; an altruistic parent; a tolerance for people who were different; the disciplining of children with an explanation of why they should act in a particular way. Quite often the adults had experienced illness or personal loss in childhood that exposed them to special care. However in some cases, especially religious homes, the fathers were stern disciplinarians. The most consistent feature was tolerance of those different from themselves. Another common characteristic of rescuers was independence of thought and also regarding their helping as natural, something that anyone would do in the circumstances. Help was usually unpremeditated – they responded to circumstances that impacted upon them.

It is not easy to estimate the scale of rescuing. The records of Yad Vashem, the Holocaust Centre in Jerusalem, now show more than 26,000 Righteous Among the Nations and the number is still growing. Miep Gies, one of those who sheltered the Frank family in Amsterdam, estimated that around 20,000 Dutch people were rescuers. If the latter is true then throughout occupied Europe there must have been a few hundred thousand. Although in some cases rescuing would involve only a single small act, in others it would be a demanding and dangerous commitment lasting years. Peter Schneider estimated that every Jew who survived required the collaboration of an average of seven non-Jewish Germans. [Anne Nelson p.293] Elizabeth Maxwell referring to the experiences of Alexander Ritenberg who crossed from France to Switzerland stated that "I find that more than fifty people were directly involved and needed in his rescue ..." [Gilbert p.15] "A Polish rescuer estimated that saving a single Jew required the support of at least ten people: an organising unit, neighbours, people who would give shelter, and those who were involved in transfers." [Oliner p.98] However in the case of diplomats the ratio could be very different as one person could sign thousands of visas.

Among religious groups (and most people at that time had religious affiliations) Roman Catholics may have played a relatively greater role in rescue than Protestants due to the availability of monasteries and convents as hiding places. Pinchas Lapide in *The Last Three Popes and the Jews* claimed that 860,000 Jews were saved by Roman Catholics.

Philip Friedman (*Their Brothers' Keepers*) estimated that of the approximately two million Jews who survived the Nazi occupation about one million had been helped by non-Jews.

SOME MORAL DILEMMAS

The abnormal circumstances that people found themselves in during the Nazi era often led to moral dilemmas. For example was it acceptable to employ lies and deception to protect oneself, or to protect others ? If one joined the underground resistance it was essential to lead a clandestine existence, and if one sheltered Jews or others sought by the security police it was probably unavoidable that one use methods that would not be considered acceptable by the same person in a free society. Rescuers felt particularly acute conflict if they had to lie to their children or teach them to lie. Lying and stealing and bribing were accepted as necessary in exceptional circumstances. Under the totalitarian system they found themselves in it is difficult to see a way out of this for those who considered they had to offer resistance or help to rescue those in peril. Theresa Weerstra as a Christian was greatly troubled by the lies and deception she used in her rescuing work and continually asked herself whether particular lies were justified.

Marion van Binsbergen Pritchard, a student in Amsterdam, was riding her bicycle when she passed in front of a Jewish children's home and saw young children being loaded onto a truck by Germans. When the crying children did not move fast enough they were grabbed by an arm or leg, or even their hair, and thrown into the truck. Then two women approached and protested at the treatment of the children but they too were thrown into a truck. So van Binsbergen decided that to oppose the Nazis directly was not effective and it would need to be secretive. The Trocmés of Le Chambon dealt with the dilemma by being quite open about sheltering Jews while not giving any details that would have led to their discovery. André Trocmé was one of a relatively small number of resisters/rescuers whose nonviolence was rooted in ethical principles and the use of deception was something that deeply troubled him. Philip Hallie expresses the dilemma in this way: "The spirit of Le Chambon in those years was a strange combination of candor and concealment, of a yearning for truth and of a commitment to secrecy. They were as open as love permits in a terrible time." [Hallie p.128]

Another aspect was to what extent one should cooperate with the occupier in order to work against them. If one is in a factory, should one appear to cooperate but in fact use go-slow or sabotage production ? Or if working in basic services should one keep them going for the sake of the general population while knowing that the occupier will benefit too ? Or even more difficult, to work with the security services in order to obtain information to give to the underground workers ? Each resister had to make their own conscientious decision. As we shall see Gandhi would probably have taken a different approach to resistance.

THE SHOAH – RESISTANCE AND COLLABORATION

A particular case under the Nazis was the special situation of the Jews themselves. From the beginning there was very little concerted resistance by Jews but discrimination was initially met mainly by emigration. Many German and Austrian Jews left for the Netherlands, Belgium and France and others went overseas to Britain and north America if they had the means and were given admission.

In Poland, where the greatest number of Jews lived, Shmuel Zygelboym tried to prevent the formation of the Warsaw ghetto by pleading with his fellow Jews to refuse to comply with the German order, but he was overruled. [Zygelboym escaped from Poland and went to London but committed suicide after the ghetto uprising.] Jewish Councils (Judenräte) were established in many of the ghettos of which there were eventually around 400 and the Nazis used these to carry out their plan to eliminate the Jews. The ghettos themselves were normally in the poorest part of towns and naturally became very overcrowded and unhealthy especially as the Germans severely limited the food available. The populations in the ghettos were not homogeneous as they contained gypsies as well as Jews who had converted to Catholicism and these people were often anti-Semitic in outlook; also the eastern ghettos had western assimilated Jews settled in them and they and the more orthodox eastern Jews did not have much in common. There were in addition to the very poor majority population some who were wealthy. All this led to mistrust and demoralisation which suited the Germans.

The order to establish Jewish Councils issued from Heydrich in September 1939 and they came to be used as exclusive channels of communication in Poland, Holland, Greece, Russia and from 1944 in Hungary. The Judenrät members acted for what they thought was the good of their community – to protect and preserve it – yet their actions enabled the smoother running of the extermination process. The Councils generally drew up the lists of those for deportation and using the Jewish police they kept order and organised the round-ups when the Germans ordered it, even putting fellow Jews onto the trains. This was very useful to the Germans not just from a labour resource aspect but it also obscured the real source of the orders. The Judenrät of Warsaw employed 5,000 people running schools, welfare services, collecting taxes, post and telephone services, medical treatment, courts. However this was to serve 450,000 people and there was extreme overcrowding with around five people to a room; of 50,000 children only around 7,000 were receiving any schooling. But cultural services were well used, such as libraries, the five theatres, concerts by a symphony orchestra, and for the small number of well-to-do there were cafés and restaurants. There were also secret areas, some underground and even extending beyond the ghetto wall where people could hide and goods could be stored.

The Dutch Jewish Council reached a peak of 17,500 and ran a free meals service, social services for sick and old people, schools and employment agencies and others, but nevertheless it involved hiding the unpleasant truth from the majority. In January 1943 Jewish police in Holland were even made responsible for the evacuation of mentally retarded children.

The Councils generally considered that resistance was futile and the best they could do was make it less traumatic for fellow Jews and hope that their efforts would result in the survival of some. When Adam Czerniakov, leader of the Warsaw Judenrät, eventually realised that he had unwittingly helped in the destruction of his people, he committed suicide by cyanide on 23 July 1942. Many others committed suicide due to living conditions or to avoid deportation. Some however managed to jump off the trains and some of these survived. Following the death of Czerniakov many in the ghetto, especially on the political left, advocated resistance by refusing to obey the orders of the Jewish police but coordinated resistance proved too difficult. The SS increased their patrols in the Warsaw ghetto. By the time the deportations from the Warsaw ghetto stopped on 12 September 1942 about 300,000 people had been deported. The remainder (perhaps 30,000), especially young people, now believed they should have fought the Germans and set fire to the ghetto.

In September 1941 the Kovno ghetto in Lithuania containing 30,000 people was sealed off and 5,000 cards were delivered to the ghetto by the Germans with instructions that they should be issued to skilled workers. The Judenrät officials began distributing them but then people became aware that possession of the cards meant that they would get work and the others without cards would be killed. People then attacked the Judenrät offices and took any cards they could find. A few days later a group of Jews who were not fit for work were taken away and shot; later, others were removed and put in a hospital that was then set on fire and all perished. Then instructions were issued for all to gather for roll-call the following morning. The Jewish leaders discussed this all night and decided to comply on the grounds that some would sacrifice their lives for the sake of some others. They were selected either to live, for the time being, or to die. Nearly 10,000 were taken out of the ghetto and shot.

In Vilna the ghetto was sealed on 6 September 1941 and ten kilometres out of town mass shootings took place at pits. A small number of Jews survived the shootings and returned to the ghetto in a terrible physical and mental state and told what had happened but they were not believed as they were considered to be mentally ill. The periodic mass killings continued. On 1 October 1941 thousands of the ghetto residents were driven by Lithuanian militia at night to the ghetto gates where the Jewish police kept them confined. Some 3,000 were taken to the death pits at Ponary and others followed in the next few days. On 1 January 1942 some ghetto youth groups issued a proclamation, a New Year's Manifesto, the first anywhere to state openly that the Germans were intending to wipe out the Jews and that they needed to resist. Abba Kovner, a 23-year-old poet who had written the final version of the Manifesto, called on the ghetto inmates not to assemble for deportation. Many of the inmates refused to believe the truth. One who opposed any resistance was the Jewish police chief, Jacob Gens. Some Jews fought when the liquidation of the ghetto began and some also escaped to the woods including Kovner who survived.

In the Lodz ghetto in Poland in January 1941 strikes broke out over food and wages. It began with the cabinet makers and then tailors and textile workers joined in. The strike collapsed after a week. Rumkowsky, the head of the Judenrät, would not concede anything even when children picketed his home. In September 1942 the Germans demanded the sick, children under ten, and adults over 65. Rumkowsky reported that the Germans demanded 10,000 children and if the numbers fell short everyone in the ghetto would be deported. However some exemptions were offered – to the community leaders if they gave their cooperation. They rejected the offer. But the Jewish police and some others offered to do the job in return for exemption of their own families. In fact the Germans soon took over the task from the Jewish collaborators.

Jewish leaders sometimes hid the truth from the majority as they thought it would lead to even greater suffering to know their fate – this is what Dr Leo Baeck, former Chief Rabbi of Berlin, did in Theresienstadt. When the information did get through to those in the ghettos many did not believe the news. The relative passivity of the Jewish communities made the job of their destruction easier and this passivity of the majority sometimes infuriated other Jews. In Wladyslav Szpilman's memoirs there is the passage: "It is a disgrace to us all. We're letting them take us to our death like sheep to the slaughter. If we attacked the Germans, half a million of us, we could break out of the ghetto, or at least die honorably, not as a stain on the face of history." (Szpilman p.101) Eventually some of the Jews of the Warsaw ghetto did rise in revolt, bravely but ineffectually in practical results. During the Warsaw ghetto uprising only 16 Germans were killed and 85 wounded. The total number of fighters, which included women, was about 750 and the battle lasted for 3 weeks in April/May 1943. A number of differing ideological groups participated. The ghetto was razed to the ground.

In the Bialystock ghetto groups of young Jews fought in August 1943 but most inhabitants did not participate, indeed many were opposed to resistance thinking that it would make matters worse. They were also so used to accommodating to the oppressor that this had become normal behaviour.

The Germans used deception skilfully to prevent the Jews knowing of the ultimate aim yet word of the reality did reach them. One of the more unusual routes was through a Polish officer called Witold Pilecki who deliberately got himself arrested in September 1940 so that he could be a spy within Auschwitz. A network of men and women couriers brought in pieces to construct a secret transmitter which they kept in a part of the camp that was typhus-infested and therefore not an area that the Germans often visited. When the exterminations began in mid-May 1942 his reports were the first detailed ones to reach the outside world. The transmitter worked for 7 months and Pilecki stayed in the camp for two-and-a-half years. Pilecki's Resistance group grew from six to 500 in 18 months but there were other groups involving some thousands of inmates. He broke out of the camp in April 1943. The organisers tried to get their best operatives into offices, kitchens, stores and hospitals within the camps where conditions were better and they were more likely to survive. They tried to get as many of their people as possible into the position of 'Kapo', that is, prisoners in charge of working parties, so that brutality would be minimised.

Violent revolts in the concentration camps also were rare but a few did occur, such as in Treblinka in August 1943 when about 1000 prisoners broke out using captured grenades and guns and ran to the surrounding forest (only a few dozen escaped with their lives), and Sobibor on 14 October 1943 when some SS men were killed and over 300 prisoners escaped. At Auschwitz-Birkenau on 7 October 1944 Sonderkommandos (Jews with special privileges) with explosives, 3 hand grenades and insulated pliers revolted – three SS men were killed and Krematorium III was set on fire but 450 prisoners were killed.

One humane reason why escapes were not common from labour camps was that the escape of those able to work would have threatened the lives of those less able to survive the conditions. A mass escape on a deportation to Belzec in September 1942 took the form of loosening floorboards on the train and jumping – about two-thirds of the escapees were killed. On a number of occasions small numbers escaped by this means.

One example of non-cooperation was based on a misunderstanding of the situation. Eva Schloss recalls this experience. In Auschwitz-Birkenau a group of around 40 women were told that their showers were not working and that they had to go to another block. They did not believe this and were convinced that they were going to be gassed so they all refused to go into the shower room. Although they were shouted at and beaten with truncheons and dogs were brought and rifles were pointed at them they refused to enter – until an officer demonstrated that they were indeed just showers. (Schloss p.121)

An unusual activity which came to be viewed as a form of resistance was set up by Emmanuel Ringelblum, a historian who gathered people who would record their existence in the Warsaw ghetto and what they observed so that the truth would be available to future generations. The documentation was called Oneg Shabbat or 'The Pleasure of the Sabbath'. The documents as they were completed were buried in containers in the hope that they would be discovered after the war which indeed many of them were. Ringelblum and his family were eventually discovered in their bunker and executed on the ruins of the ghetto on 10 March 1944.

Another subtle but powerful form of resistance that took place during the deportations from the Warsaw ghetto was the manner in which the children of the orphanages departed. Dr Janucz Korczak, pediatrician and writer, refused the offer of safety in order to be with the children of the orphanages he ran in the ghetto. On the day of the deportation some 200 children dressed in their best clean clothes marched out of the orphanage in rows of four holding hands. At the head of the column was Dr Korczak holding the hand of a child on each side of him. Nachum Remba who worked as a secretary in the Jewish Council observed the departure of the children: "... throwing at the barbarian murderers facial expressions filled with a collective, uniform disdain." "... commanded by no one, the Jewish police force stood erect; soundlessly, respectfully, they saluted this dignified procession of children and their educators." [Tec p.70]

THE POTENTIAL OF NONVIOLENT RESISTANCE

Considering how much pragmatic nonviolent resistance took place – and in every occupied country – the question arises whether this could have been on a larger scale, and whether it could have been widespread enough even to have brought about regime change. The great majority of participants were not believers in nonviolent action as a morally superior way of acting but simply used methods that 'came to hand'.

A greater awareness of the potential of nonviolent resistance and the many forms it can take would seem likely to have increased the use of the method by the occupied populations. It was largely improvised responses that were used and such is the creativity of the human mind that these often were effective. But a combination of prior knowledge of nonviolent actions used at different times and places along with openness to respond to one's particular circumstances would seem likely to produce greater effectiveness. Without the cooperation of a large proportion of an occupied population a regime is unstable and in the long-run it will collapse.

On the occupying side there was much dissatisfaction among German armed forces and members of the Nazi administrative apparatus, which increased as the war progressed. Some of this expressed itself as attempts on Hitler's life and plans to end the war through negotiation with the Allies. Of course diminishing success on the battlefield was no doubt a major factor in this change but difficulty in controlling a determined civilian population can produce the same effect.

There was even some resistance by individual members of the SS who refused to take part in executions of Jews. A former Wehrmacht psychiatrist who had treated members of the Einstazgruppen killing squads considered that 20% of the men suffered from severe anxiety, nightmares, tremors and numerous physical complaints. Obergruppenfuhrer Bach-Zelewski, an officer with the squads, himself became ill and suffered from visions of the killings. [Glover, p.345] Closeness to the individuals being executed did affect some individual executioners and so Gandhi's belief that undeserved suffering would have an effect on those inflicting it is at least true in some cases. Remarkably, no instance has been found of refusals to take part in such actions resulting in execution. Historian Daniel Goldhagen investigated 100 cases of Nazis who refused to participate in the shooting or gassing of Jews or others and found that nothing happened to them other than being transferred to other duties. A few members of the SS personally helped Jews as mentioned earlier.

Gene Sharp, an American academic who has systematised nonviolent action found 198 different methods used and has grouped them as Protest and Persuasion, Intervention, and Non-cooperation in its Social, Economic and Political forms. Examples of all of these can be found in resistance to the Nazis.

Protest and Persuasion often includes the use of symbols. Displaying significant colours such as national colours in different ways was a common expression of protest in the occupied countries of western Europe. Paperclips on lapels signifying 'holding together' was one of many used by the Danes. Graffiti on walls and leafletting were used by the White Rose resisters in German cities. Singing of patriotic songs lifted the spirits of the singers as well as signifying defiance. Marches on significant dates or simply gathering on an important date were important especially in France. Listening to unapproved radio broadcasts was a common but clandestine activity as was the production of underground newspapers and their distribution which was done on a large scale. The 'V' symbol as signifying victory was proposed by the BBC's Belgium programme organiser in 1941, was adopted by the BBC and then spread throughout the occupied countries.

Intervention included the release by various methods of those detained and in danger of deportation including provision of false passes, also hiding and transporting those in danger. Letters of protest to officials of the occupying power were used, particularly by religious leaders in eastern Europe as well as in the west. The letters were very often kept private but it was discovered in time that open letters received more attention by the government officials. Intervention included actions to release those incarcerated such as the release of deportees on a train in Rumania. There were also the many rescue groups which took escapees across borders to neutral countries like Sweden, Switzerland and Spain. There was the provision of alternative services such as the remarkable underground universities and schools developed especially in Poland.

Social non-cooperation was probably less common than the other forms of non-cooperation but one that was used was deliberately ignoring individual members of the occupying force, a form of ostracism. Another type was boycotting of events or institutions, for example, in Norway no sports events took place during the occupation and theatres closed.

While there are instances of individuals acting entirely alone – and presumably there were others not recorded – acting in a group generally helps to reduce the fear of acting against the authorities. The larger the group the lower the fear as the risk is perceived as being lessened for any one individual.

Economic non-cooperation gave more scope for action but also carried more risk. There were general strikes in Belgium, the Netherlands and France but they only lasted for a few days. Strikes also took place on the railways and in mines in France and Belgium. Refusal to be conscripted for the army or labour abroad was widespread. Going-slow at work or making deliberate mistakes was common.

Political non-cooperation included refusal to carry out orders, refusal to take an oath of loyalty to the regime as the Norwegian teachers and clergy did, and as did staff at the Cévenol school in Le Chambon-sur-Lignon. Some civil servants and others resigned from their posts, and there were refusals to attend regime events such as the appointment of Quisling in Trondheim Cathedral. Political noncooperation included refusing compulsory registration for various purposes.

The mechanisms operating when such methods are used can be one of three types: conversion, accommodation and nonviolent coercion. The first is the one that Gandhi favoured as he believed that the suffering endured by the satyagrahi (participant in a satyagraha) would 'melt the heart' of the opponent and convert him/her. However even in his own campaigns the other mechanisms were operative. The exercise of power is present even in an ethically driven campaign. But it should not be entirely coercive, there should be a recognition that the opponent is a human being with the possibility of changing. Even if the most dedicated Nazi would be very unlikely to weaken their stance that would not be true of many of the rank-and-file who when met by courageous nonviolence would be likely to be affected.

Sharp says that effective nonviolent coercion can "take place in any of three ways:

- The defiance becomes too widespread and massive to be controlled by the opponents' repression and other means of control.
- The noncooperation and the defiance make it impossible for the social, economic and political system to operate unless the resisters' demands are achieved.
- Even the opponents' ability to apply repression is undermined or dissolved because their own forces for applying repression (police or military) become unreliable or disintegrate."

[Sharp, *Waging Nonviolent Struggle* p.418]

This stage was not achieved across a whole country but in some sectors, such as the Norwegian teachers, it was.

It is also the case that there are not usually just two actors involved in a conflict. External circumstances will usually impact too. In the case of the women of Berlin and their Jewish husbands the effects of the action on the wider German population had to be taken account of by the regime.

One can see that it is possible to use nonviolent resistance against a Nazi-type regime. The form that resistance took varied depending on the interaction between the particular country and population and the nature of the imposed regime.

Types of Nonviolent Action Used Against the Nazis and Select Examples

PROTEST & PERSUASION

Wearing symbols including significant colours – Denmark, Norway, Netherlands, France, Czechoslovakia

Marches, sometimes on significant dates – France

Rallies & pilgrimages, sometimes including singing – Denmark, Netherlands, Czechoslovakia, Bulgaria

Attendance at funerals of opponents of the Nazis – Channel Islands, Czechoslovakia, Denmark

Stay at home – Czechoslovakia

Leaflet, poster & graffiti distribution – White Rose Germany, V-sign in most countries

Telling of anti-German jokes and spreading rumours

Letters of protest, private & public – parents & teachers in Norway; letters from clergy – Germany (RC opposition to T4, opposition to Nazification of Church), Belgium (Cardinal Roey opposing forced labour), France, Netherlands (CIC Army signs declaration of independence), Bulgaria (pro-Jews)

INTERVENTION

Freeing political prisoners or Jews – Belgium, France, Poland

Hiding those being sought by the Nazis

Underground press – France, Belgium, Netherlands, Poland
Listening to radio – everywhere
Supplying documents to the persecuted – diplomats in France,
Netherlands,
Strikes for improved conditions – France, Belgium

SOCIAL NON-COOPERATION

Ostracising occupiers' agents – Denmark, Norway
Refusal to wear yellow star – individual Jews
Boycotting theatre, cinema, concerts, sports events – Norway,
Denmark, Czechoslovakia
Strike by actors – Norway

ECONOMIC NON-COOPERATION

Refusing to be conscripted for work – Belgium, Luxemburg, France
Sabotaging manufactures – widespread
Slow working – Belgium (coal miners), Czechoslavakia (factories),
widespread
Refusal to work – Denmark (repair German ships), Belgium (teaching)

POLITICAL NON-COOPERATION

Resigning from posts – Belgium (judges), Netherlands (Leyden
University staff), Norway (Supreme Court, Bishops)
Refusing to join official organisations –Netherlands (doctors),
Norway (doctors, teachers),
Refusals of oaths of loyalty to regime – Norway (teachers), Belgian
universities, Netherlands (students and artists & actors)

Refusing to be deported – Netherlands general strikes (former soldiers, Jews)

Refusing to be conscripted – Luxemburg

Refusing to surrender Jews – Finland

Refusing to register – Netherlands (doctors), Norway (for labour)

Refusal to enter ghettos voluntarily

Continuing to work outside of official bodies – Norway (doctors, clergy, teachers),

Census used as protest – Luxemburg

CONSTRUCTIVE ACTION

Hiding/rescuing – every country

German officials informing of round-ups

Escaping – Danish Jews and other small groups to neutral countries, passes supplied by diplomats (Hungary, Czechoslovakia, France, Austria, Lithuania)

Relief funds – Netherlands, Poland, France

Funds from abroad – Governments-in-Exile, and the Joint (American)

Establishing Underground institutions – Poland (educational, judicial, governmental, social), Norway (teaching), Belgium (teaching), Netherlands (Leyden University)

A Gandhian Approach

The greatest exponent of nonviolent action, Mohandas K Gandhi, developed a form of nonviolent action which he called *satyagraha* (holding firmly to the truth). This had an ethical foundation derived from various sources including the Jain religion, Jesus and Tolstoy and modern collective action such as labour strikes and the suffragists' campaign. It was first used by Gandhi in South Africa with the Indian community there in defence of their civil rights. Gandhi continued to develop his understanding of satyagraha throughout his life until assassinated by a Hindu at the age of 78 in 1948.

The use of satyagraha against the Japanese army who threatened India during the Second World War was advocated by Gandhi but the Japanese invasion did not materialise and he did not have the opportunity to develop in any detail his ideas on how to respond to a foreign occupation. But it is useful to see if Gandhi's ethical approach would have produced a significantly different form of resistance from those used in Nazi occupied Europe.

For Gandhi, truth was the fundamental principle of life. On this one cannot imagine a greater contrast than Gandhi and Hitler. For the latter, truth meant nothing and power over others everything. Immediately we see a great difference from most of the resistance used in Europe against the Nazis. The underground was underpinned by secrecy, forged documents were produced on a huge scale, lies were told in the hope of saving lives. All of this seems to go against Gandhi's principle. Openness would have produced a very different resistance. Gandhi believed the means used will determine the end achieved and so one cannot use wrong means even although the cause is good. Individual resisters in his campaigns were to harbour no anger and be prepared to suffer for the truth. Gandhi also placed courage high among the virtues and this characteristic was something that the historical resisters to the Nazis shared. Another thing expected of satyagrahis was refusal to submit to unjust or humiliating orders.

British moral philosopher Howard Horsburgh in his *Non-violence and Aggression* considers some tactics advocated by other writers on foreign occupation such as scorched earth policy (eg Jessie W Hughan and Cecil Hinshaw in *Towards a Non-violent National Defense*); also barring the invader's advance by bodily obstruction, both of which Gandhi criticised. There are objections to the first tactic on humanitarian grounds and also because scorched earth policy would insulate the invader from the invaded and reduce contacts which are desirable for a resolution of the conflict. Gandhi did not rule out completely barring the route of the invader but in practice soldiers can be landed behind the frontline by air so its relevance is in doubt. The most suitable tactic is noncooperation with the invader but not total noncooperation as this is difficult to maintain, rather limited noncooperation by different sectors of the population, and also phasing them to make resistance easier to maintain over a protracted period. This leaves room for negotiation and the initiative is retained by the resisters. This contrasts with the violent aggressor and the violent defender where military defeat is uppermost in the minds of both sides and negotiation is mostly absent.

Gandhi believed that satyagraha offered a substitute for conflict of all kinds. Regarding the extreme form of conflict, namely, war, Horsburgh borrowed an expression by the American philosopher William James – the 'Moral Equivalent of War' and applied it to Gandhi's satyagraha. Horsburgh pointed out that the effectiveness of violence relies on coercion alone in contrast to nonviolence which involves conversion and concession as well as some degree of coercion.

Gandhi's attitude to the plight of the Jews, and to dissident non-Jews, can be seen in the extracts below which appeared in his journal *Harijan*.

But the German persecution of the Jews seems to have no parallel in history. The tyrants of old never went so mad as Hitler seems to have gone. And he is doing it with religious zeal. For, he is propounding a new religion of exclusive and militant nationalism in the name of which any inhumanity becomes an act of humanity to be rewarded here and hereafter. The crime of an obviously mad but intrepid youth is being visited upon his whole race with unbelievable ferocity. [This appears to be a reference to Jewish student Hershl Grynszpan whose murder of a German diplomat in Paris led to the Krystallnacht pogrom. GP] *If ever there could be a justifiable war in the name of and for humanity, a war against Germany, to prevent the wanton persecution of a whole race, would be completely justified. But I do not believe in any war.*

... Can the Jews resist this organised and shameless persecution? Is there a way to preserve their self-respect, and not to feel helpless or forlorn. I submit that there is.

... If I were a Jew and were born in Germany and earned my livelihood there, I would claim Germany as my home even as the tallest gentile German might, and challenge him to shoot me or cast me in the dungeon; I would refuse to be expelled or to submit to discriminating treatment. And for doing this I should not wait for the Jews to join me in civil resistance, but would have confidence that in the end the rest were bound to follow my example. If one Jew or all the Jews were to accept the prescription here offered, he or they cannot be worse off than now. And suffering voluntarily undergone will bring them an inner strength and joy which no number of resolutions of sympathy passed in the world outside Germany can.

... the Jews of Germany can offer Satyagraha under infinitely better auspices than the Indians of South Africa. The Jews are a compact homogeneous community in Germany. They are far more gifted than the Indians of South Africa. And they have organized world opinion behind them. I am convinced that, if someone with courage and vision can arise among them to lead them in non-violent

action, the winter of their despair can in the twinkling of an eye be turned into the summer of hope. And what today has become a degrading man-hunt can be turned into a calm and determined stand offered by unarmed men and women possessing the strength of suffering given to them by Jehovah. It will be then a truly religious resistance offered against the godless fury of dehumanized man. The German Jews will score a lasting victory over the German gentiles in the sense that they will have converted the latter to an appreciation of human dignity. They will have rendered service to fellow-Germans and proved their title to be the real Germans as against those who are today dragging, however unknowingly, the German name into the mire.

Harijan 26/11/1938 [Non-violence in Peace & War Vol I, pp.171-3]

I do not think that the sufferings of Pastor Niemoeller and others have been in vain. They have preserved their self-respect intact. They have proved that their faith was equal to any suffering. That they have not proved sufficient for melting Herr Hitler's heart merely shows that it is made of harder stuff than stone. But the hardest metal yields to sufficient heat. Even so must the hardest heart melt before sufficiency of the heat of nonviolence. And there is no limit to the capacity of nonviolence to generate heat.

... Herr Hitler is but one man enjoying no more than the average span of life. He would be a spent force, if he had not the backing of his people. I do not despair of his responding to human suffering even though caused by him. But I must refuse to believe that the Germans as a nation have no heart or markedly less than the other nations of the earth. They will some day or other rebel against their own adored hero, if he does not wake up betimes. And when he or they do, we shall find that the sufferings of the Pastor and his fellow-workers had not a little to do with the awakening.

Harijan 7/1/1939 [Non-violence in Peace & War Vol I, p.191]

Gandhi's answer to invasion can be seen from the following extracts from his journal *Harijan*:

... Hitlerism will never be defeated by counter-Hitlerism. It can only breed superior Hitlerism raised to nth degree. What is going on before our eyes is a demonstration of the futility of violence as also of Hitlerism.

... As against this imagine the state of Europe today if the Czechs, the Poles, the Norwegians, the French and the English had all said to Hitler: "You need not make your scientific preparation for destruction. We will meet your violence with non-violence. You will, therefore, be able to destroy our non-violent army without tanks, battleships and airships." It may be retorted that the only difference would be that Hitler would have got without fighting what he has gained after a bloody fight. Exactly. The history of Europe would then have been written differently. Possession might (but only might) have been then taken under non-violent resistance, as it has been taken now after perpetration of untold barbarities. Under non-violence only those would have been killed who had trained themselves to be killed, if need be, but without killing anyone and without bearing malice towards anybody. I dare say that in that case Europe would have added several inches to its moral stature. And in the end I expect it is the moral worth that will count. All else is dross.

Harijan 22/6/1940 [Non-violence in Peace & War Vol I, p.290]

I appeal [to every Briton] for cessation of hostilities, not because you are too exhausted to fight, but because war is bad in essence. You want to kill Nazism. You will never kill it by its indifferent adoption. Your soldiers are doing the same work of destruction as the Germans. The only difference is that perhaps yours are not as thorough as the Germans. If that be so, yours will soon acquire the same thoroughness as theirs, if not much greater. On no other condition can you win the war. In other words, you will have to be more ruthless than the Nazis.

No cause, however just, can warrant the indiscriminate slaughter that is going on minute by minute. I suggest that a cause that demands the inhumanities that are being perpetrated today cannot be called just.

... I want you to fight Nazism without arms, or if I am to retain the military terminology, with non-violent arms. I would like you to lay down the arms you have as being useless for saving your humanity. You will invite Herr Hitler and Signor Mussolini to take what they want of the countries you call your possessions. Let them take possession of your beautiful island, with your many beautiful buildings. You will give all these but neither your souls, nor your minds. If these gentlemen choose to occupy your homes, you will vacate them. If they do not give you free passage out, you will allow yourselves man, woman and child, to be slaughtered, but you will refuse to owe allegiance to them.
Harijan 6/7/1940 [Nonviolence in Peace & War, Vol I, pp.296-7)

Why should the Appeal [to Britain] breed any ill-will at all? There is no cause given for it by the manner or the matter of the Appeal. I have not advised cessation of fight. I have advised lifting it to a plane worthy of human nature, of the divinity man shares with God Himself. If the hidden meaning of the remarks is that by making the Appeal I have strengthened Nazi hands, the suggestion does not bear scrutiny. Herr Hitler can only be confounded by the adoption by Britain of the novel method of fighting. At one single stroke he will find that all his tremendous armament has been put out of action. A warrior lives on his wars whether offensive or defensive. He suffers a collapse, if he finds that his warring capacity is unwanted.
Harijan 28/7/1940 [Nonviolence in Peace & War Vol I, p.322]

Japan is knocking at our gates. What are we to do in a non-violent way? If we were a free country, things could be done non-violently to prevent he Japanese from entering the country. As it is, non-violent resistance could commence the moment they effected a landing. Thus non-violent resisters would refuse them any help, even water. For it

is no part of their duty to help anyone to steal their country. But if a Japanese has missed his way and was dying of thirst and sought help as a human being, a non-violent resister, who may not regard anyone as his enemy, would give water to the thirsty one. Suppose the Japanese compel resisters to give them water, the resisters must die in the act of resistance. It is conceivable that they will exterminate all resisters. The underlying belief in such non-violent resistance is that the aggressor will, in time, be mentally and even physically tired of killing non-violent resisters. He will begin to search what this new (for him) force is which refuses co-operation without seeking to hurt, and will probably desist from further slaughter. But the resisters may find that the Japanese are utterly heartless and that they do not care how many they kill. The non-violent resisters will have won the day inasmuch as they will have preferred extermination to submission.
Harijan 12/4/1942 [Nonviolence in Peace & War Vol I, p.417]

Gandhi believed in the power of undeserved suffering to melt the heart of the opponent. Few would go along with him in the case of the Jews facing the insane ideology of the Nazi Party and its leaders. Two prominent Jews were very disappointed by Gandhi's advice to the German Jews: Martin Buber, the famous Jewish philosopher who had escaped from Germany, and Rabbi Judah Magnes, who was from the Reform tradition in the USA and became Rector of the Hebrew University in Jerusalem; Magnes was also a pacifist who was driven to give up this belief in the face of Nazism. Both thought Gandhi had no conception of the extreme circumstances that the Jews of Europe were in and objected to his drawing a parallel between the Indians in South Africa and the Jews in Germany. Unfortunately although both wrote to Gandhi in 1939 no reply from him exists and he may not have seen the letters.

While Gandhi emphasised in his writings on this issue the willingness of the Jews (and others) to suffer he certainly believed that the opponents of the Nazis should also actively resist the oppressors. Perhaps he was reluctant to admit that his own campaigns did often have a coercive element. He did believe that displaying cowardice was worse than killing in a just cause but nonviolence of the brave was greatly to be preferred. Nonviolent action used with courage and persistence, and imagination, can achieve desired results as can be seen in many of the actions described earlier. If nonviolent coercion is part of the process this is at least much more to be desired than violent coercion. Of course NVR does not inevitably lead to success any more than the use of violence does but Chenoweth and Stephan showed that nonviolent campaigns were twice as likely to succeed than campaigns using armed force. There is also probably reduced risk to the participants because the nature of the actions reduces the threat to the opponent who are then likely to be less violent.

Sometimes in specific circumstances there is little hope of effective resistance and in such circumstances to respond with dignity and defiance can matter, as in the case of the children of the Warsaw ghetto orphanage described earlier. Another instance is given by Evelyn Wilcock in *Pacifism and the Jews* (p.164):

'*Are you still the Chosen people, Herr Rabbiner ?*' demanded a Nazi officer in Bergen Belsen after knocking down the Klausenberger Rebbe. '*Zicher, to be sure. As long as we are not the oppressors, we are the Chosen people.*'

Let us try to imagine a Gandhian resistance to the Nazi regime and see how different it would have been from pragmatic NVR which tended to respond to specific situations without having an overall strategy.

In addition to adhering to truth and nonviolence, Gandhi advised that one should never allow oneself to be humiliated. The Germans were systematic in their attempt to eliminate the Jews. The stages gone through were:

- identification by compulsory registration
- exclusion from the professions
- dispossession of property
- exclusion from public places
- marking with the Yellow Star
- regrouping into ghettos
- setting up Jewish Councils
- round-ups
- deportation
- forced labour
- extermination.

Not all of these stages were necessarily present in all countries, for example the Jewish Star was not introduced in Italy or in Vichy France, and in Hungary only when the Germans occupied the country, nor in Bulgaria which had a yellow button which was then abandoned; many Jews were not put into ghettos and not all did forced labour.

With the advantage of hindsight we can see that resistance should have come into operation at the earliest stage, something which would have followed from Gandhi's advice not to accept humiliating treatment. The Nazis cleverly reduced the impact of restrictions by going through many stages which the Jews could persuade themselves would be the last. The Jews should have refused to register in the first place; they should have refused to wear the Yellow Star; they should have refused to go to ghettos voluntarily; they should have refused to serve on the Jewish Councils under German control; they should not have provided the Jewish police; they should have refused to work for the Germans in factories or in the construction industry. The Germans deliberately tried to mislead the Jews as to their aim as it made it easier for them if they said, for example, that those deported were going to work camps, or that the ghettos were going to be run by fellow Jews.

But Gandhi would have been firm – no cooperation with acts that humiliated, no matter the cost. If the Jews had been able to show such courage it would have been much more difficult for the Germans to achieve their aim. It is true that the individual resister would have put their life at risk but collectively they would have been much stronger. They would have refused to leave their homes voluntarily. They would have refused to get into cattle trucks on rail or on to lorries. They could have arranged themselves into lines and refused to move, perhaps sitting down. So much of the interaction between oppressors and oppressed, occupiers and occupied was hidden – the rescuers and the resisters constituted the underground, and the occupiers tried to hide the reality of the extermination process from the victims. A Gandhian approach is that the resistance should be public as far as possible so that everyone can see what is happening and if the observers (both occupiers and bystanders) are not personally in danger their consciences would be challenged by the situation.

Some Jews did urge non-cooperation with the Nazis as we saw. The resisters – non-Jewish and sometimes Jewish – had the advantage of superior numbers and if they had acted with solidarity also they would have made it very difficult for the oppressors. The non-Jewish population should have come to the Jews' aid, as indeed some did, for example, students protesting against dismissal of professors, Jews being freed from locked cattle trucks. Much more of this was needed.

Regarding defence and noncooperation by the general population, it is necessary for the populace to be selective in their actions as they require for their existence food and other supplies such as water and electricity and health services. There would be refusal to be conscripted for work. The exporting of manufactured goods and food to Germany, which was on a vast scale, should have been resisted. Immediately after the defeat of France the Germans demanded of the French Government occupation costs of 146 billion francs which was estimated by French General Charles Huntziger as sufficient to maintain an army of 18 million men. French workers were the main food suppliers of the Germans but Danish farmers exported to Germany more than was requested by the Germans, for example, in 1944 the Danes exported enough to feed 8.4 million Germans.

Refusal to help in the manufacture and transport of arms would be non-negotiable. The potential strength of the Jews in Poland is indicated by the numbers in war industries. Over a million workers were in war production factories for the Germans with about 30% of them being Jewish. Lodz had a Jewish population of 160,000 and Jews worked in 117 factories, workshops and warehouses at the peak of production. Is there not a certain irony in these large numbers of men and women working daily for their exterminators? It is clear that the exploitation of the occupied countries' resources was an essential part of the German war machine. However there were some rare cases of employers protecting Jews in their workforce. Oscar Schindler's factory produced goods for the German forces and managed to protect 700 Jews, while Berthold Beitz, whose company developed oil fields in Galicia, protected some hundreds of Jews with the help of his wife and some colleagues. Nevertheless they were still aiding the Germans too.

Diderich Lund, a nonviolent Norwegian resister, recalled: "In the economic field our resistance broke down completely, although it soon became clear that every economic activity authorised by the Germans was intended to aid their war effort, even so humble and innocent an activity as growing potatoes. Norwegian men of business, contractors and workmen offered their services to the invader, and continued to do so throughout the war, in spite of strong agitation directed against it by the resistance leaders". [Lund p357] Yet it was always an option for people to refuse. Louisa Steenstra who worked in a Jewish owned factory in Groningen refused to work there, at some risk, when the factory was taken over by Germans. She became a rescuer driven by the fury aroused in her by the bombing of Rotterdam and their other foul deeds.

Civil servants would need to draw the line also. None of the occupied countries could have been held without a great deal of bureaucratic cooperation.

Resistance by the general population included:

- wearing symbols of resistance
- listening to radio broadcasts and refusing to surrender radios
- writing letters of protest to relevant departments
- distributing posters and leaflets
- taking part in demonstrations
- setting up means of communication eg newspapers
- refusal of police to apply Nazi orders
- refusing to register for work in Germany
- refusing to work in weapons' factories
- refusing to take Nazi oaths
- refusing to join Nazi organisations
- expressing solidarity with Jews

These did occur – but they needed to be done by more people; with more coordination.

The Gandhian approach would have involved resistance being open, not underground, and this would have resulted in a substantially different appearance to the resistance. For example, it would have involved a direct appeal to the humanity of the enforcers of the occupation, as well as bystanders. Whether a Gandhian approach or less scrupulous nonviolent methods of resistance would be more effective has still to be demonstrated. In reality a mixture of both is likely to be used.

Countries outside of Nazi control have a role also using nonviolent actions. Trade sanctions should be aimed at weakening the military prowess of the enemy without at the same time severely affecting the occupied populations, although not an easy effect to achieve. Weapons would obviously be excluded but oil or other goods which could be of dual use are more problematic. A food embargo would most likely affect the general population more than the occupying power so should probably be excluded. Countries with a diverse economy are probably more resilient than those dependent on fewer products which need to be traded outside of the country.

Access to finance should be denied to the occupier if possible but the occupied should be aided and this actually proved possible during the war through the governments-in-exile and other sources whose links to those under occupation allowed transfer across state boundaries even when these states were at war with each other.

Broadcasts to the occupied countries of Europe, mainly by the BBC in the different languages of Europe, were eagerly listened to by the occupied peoples and were of great importance for morale.

Refusing passage to troops of the belligerents across the territory of a neutral state should be obvious yet in the case of Sweden this did happen, although one has to acknowledge the important role Sweden had in welcoming those escaping from Reich territory. In general taking in refugees from the occupied countries was of great importance yet all receiving countries placed limits on the numbers including the large belligerents of Britain and its Empire and the USA.

Conclusion

The Nazi era revealed the very worst aspects of human nature. Survivor of the Shoah, Eva Schloss, in her Preface to *Eva's Story* wrote: "My posthumous step-sister, Anne Frank, wrote in her *Diary*: 'I still believe that deep down human beings are good at heart.' I cannot help remembering that she wrote this *before* she experienced Auschwitz and Belsen." Human beings can sink to appalling depths of depravity – history reveals such and we can see it today. But the extreme challenges arising out of the Nazi era and the Second World War also brought out the best in other people. In spite of the likelihood of imprisonment, or worse, if detected helping Jews many thousands of rescuers were prepared to come to the aid of complete strangers. This aid often extended to years of concealment at extreme inconvenience for the helpers and involved obtaining identity papers and ration books with considerable difficulty, delivering food and praying that none of the concealed individuals would fall ill. Resisters too, for example those distributing underground newspapers or refusing to work for the Nazis, were at great risk. The activists greatly varied in their circumstances: professional and business people, factory workers and farmers, those who were well off and those who had very little, Protestants and Catholics, atheists and Quakers, married and unmarried, with children and without – people of diverse backgrounds and beliefs. Yet they were willing to risk everything in support of freedom or to save other human beings who were often strangers to them.

It also reveals that even in exceptionally difficult circumstances nonviolent action can be used and be effective. And if it can be used in such circumstances it can be used more generally in situations of conflict. It is also clearly the case that the kind of society we find ourselves born into can greatly affect our mental outlook and actions – the majority were influenced by whether the society was predominantly fascist or democratic, anti-semitic or tolerant, militaristic or peaceable. It is therefore up to all of us to work to create a society that encourages humane and just values – and gives a prominent place to nonviolence. The latter would mean a reassessment of the concept of security with practical changes to follow.

Bibliography

Arendt, Hannah, *Eichmann in Jerusalem: A Report on the Banality of Evil,* Penguin 1994

Bentley, James, *Martin Niemöller,* Hodder & Stoughton 1984

Bierman, John, *Righteous Gentile,* Penguin 2001

Bondurant, Joan, *The Conquest of Violence,* Princeton University Press 1958

Boserup, Anders and Andrew Mack, *War without Weapons,* Frances Pinter 1974

Brittain, Vera, *The Rebel Passion,* George Allen & Unwin 1964

Brock, Peter and Nigel Young, *Pacifism in the Twentieth Century,* Syracuse University Press 1999

Brock, Peter and Thomas P Socknat Editors, *Challenge to Mars: Essays on Pacifism from 1918 to 1945,* University of Toronto Press 1999

Bunting, Madeleine, *The Model Occupation: The Channel Islands under German Rule 1940-1945,* Harper Collins 1995

Burrowes, Robert J, *The Strategy of Nonviolent Defense: A Gandhian Approach,* State University of New York Press 1996

Chenoweth, Erica and Maria J Stephan, *Why Civil Resistance Works: The Strategic Logic of Nonviolent Conflict,* Columbia University Press 2013

Cohen, Maynard M, *A Stand Against Tyranny: Norway's Physicians and the Nazis,* Wayne State University Press 1997

Cornwell, John, *Hitler's Pope: The Secret History of Pius XII*, Penguin 2000

Cornwell, John, *Hitler's Scientists: Science, War and the Devil's Pact*, Penguin 2004

Dawidowicz, Lucy, *The War Against the Jews 1933-45,* Penguin 1977

Dumback, Annette & Jud Newborn, *Sophie Scholl and the White Rose,* One World Publications Oxford 2006

Eman, Diet, *Things We Couldn't Say,* William B Eerdmans, Michigan 1994

Fogelman, Eva, *Conscience and Courage: Rescuers of Jews During the Holocaust,* Anchor Books 1995

Fralon, José-Alain, *A Good Man in Evil Times,* Penguin 1982

Frank, Otto and Miriam Pressler Eds, Trans. Susan Massotty *Anne Frank: The Diary of a Young Girl,* Viking 1997

Gandhi, M K, *Non-violence in Peace and War,* Navajivan Publishing House Vol. 1, 1942; Vol. 2, 1949

Gilbert, Martin, *The Righteous: The Unsung Heroes of the Holocaust,* Black Swan 2002

Gilbert, Martin, *Atlas of the Holocaust,* Michael Joseph 1982

Glover, Jonathan, *Humanity: A Moral History of the 20th Century,* Yale University Press, 2nd Edition 2012

Grunwald-Spier, Agnes, *The Other Schindlers*, The History Press 2011

Haffner, Sebastan, *Defying Hitler,* Phoenix 2002

Hallie, Philip, *Lest Innocent Blood be Shed,* Harper Perennial 1994

Hilberg, Raul, *The Destruction of the European Jews,* 3 vols Chicago 1961

Hilberg, Raul, *Perpetrators, Victims, Bystanders: The Jewish Catastrophe 1933-45,* Harper Perennial 1993

Horsburgh, H J N, *Non-violence and Aggression: A Study of Gandhi's Moral Equivalent of War,* Oxford University Press 1968

Housden, Martyn, *Resistance and Conformity in the Third Reich,* Routledge 1997

Janfeldt, Bengt, *The Hero of Budapest,* I B Tauris 2014

Kassow, Samuel D, *Who Will Write Our History?,* Penguin 2007

Lev, Shimon, "'Can the Jews Resist this organised and shameless persecution?" Gandhi's Attitude to the Holocaust', *Gandhi Marg* Vol. 35 No. 3 Oct-Dec 2013

Levi, Primo, *If This is a Man & The Truce*, Abacus 1987

Light, Bart de, *The Conquest of Violence*, Pluto Press 1989

Lund, Diderich H, 'Pacifism under the Occupation', *The Pacifist Conscience* Ed by Peter Mayer, Penguin 1966

Martin, Brian, 'The Nazis and nonviolence', *Social Alternatives* Vol. 6 No. 3 August 1987 pp.47-49

Melchior, Marcus, *Darkness over Denmark,* New English Library, London 1973

Moorehead, Caroline, *Village of Secrets; Defying the Nazis in Vichy France,* Chatto & Windus 2014

Nagler, Michael N, *The Search for a Nonviolent Future,* New World Library, California 2004

Nelson, Anne, *Red Orchestra,* Random House, New York 2009

Oliner, Samuel P and Pearl M Oliner, *The Altruistic Personality: Rescuers of Jews in Nazi Europe,* The Free Press, New York 1988

Overy, Richard, *The Penguin Historical Atlas of the Third Reich,* London 1996

Paulsson, Gunnar S, *Secret City: The Hidden Jews of Warsaw 1940-45,* Yale University Press 2002

Prasad, Devi, *War is a Crime against Humanity: The Story of War Resisters' International,* War Resisters' International, London 2005

Putz, Erna, *Franz Jägerstätter: A Shining Example in Dark Times,* Buchverlag Franz Steinmassi 2007

Ramati, Alexander, *The Assisi Underground*, Unwin Paperbacks, London 1985

Rings, Werner, *Life with the Enemy: Collaboration and Resistance in Hitler's Europe 1939-1945*, Doubleday 1982

Rittner, Carol, Stephen D Smith and Irena Sreinfeldt, *The Holocaust and the Christian World*, Kuperard, London 2000

Roberts, Adam, Editor, *Civilian Resistance as a National Defence*, Penguin 1969

Scholl, Inga, *The White Rose; Munich 1942-1943*, Wesleyan University Press 2nd edition 1983

Semelin, Jacques, Trans. Suzan Husserl-Kapit, *Unarmed Against Hitler: Civilian Resistance in Europe 1939-43*, Praeger, London 1993

Sharp, Gene, 'The Lesson of Eichmann', *Social Power and Political Freedom*, Porter Sargent 1980

Sharp, Gene, *The Politics of Nonviolence* 3 Vols, Porter Sargent, Boston 1973

Sharp, Gene, *Tyranny Could not Quell Them*, Peace News, London 1958

Sharp, Gene, *Waging Nonviolent Struggle: 20th Century Practice, 21st Century Potential*, Porter Sargent, Boston 2005

Shatzkes, Pamela, *Holocaust and Rescue: Impotent or Indifferent? 1938-1945*, Vallentine Mitchell 2002

Sibley, Mulford Q, Edited by, *The Quiet Battle,* Anchor Books 1963

Smith, Lyn, *Heroes of the Holocaust,* Ebury Press 2013

Stratford, Michael C, 'Can nonviolent defence be effective if the opponents are ruthless?: The Nazi case', *Social Alternatives* Vol. 6 No. 2 April 1987 pp.49-57

Stratford, Michael C, 'The Nazis and nonviolent defence', *Social Alternatives* Vol. 8 No. 3 Oct 1989 pp.58-61

Summy, Ralph, 'Defending nonviolent defence', *Social Alternatives* Vol. 6 No. 3 August 1987 pp.49-50

Szpilman, Wladyslaw, *The Pianist,* Orion Books 2005

Stoltzfus, Nathan, 'Dissent in Nazi Germany' , *The Atlantic Monthly* September 1992

Straede, Therkel, *October 1943: the Rescue of the Danish Jews from Annihilation,* Royal Danish Ministry of Foreign Affairs 1993

Synnestvedt, Alice Resch, *Over the Highest Mountains,* International Productions, Pasadena 2005

Tec, Nechama, *Resistance: Jews and Christians Who Defied the Nazi Terror,* Oxford University Press 2013

Wallenburg, Raoul, *Letters and Dispatches 1924-1944,* Arcade Publishing, New York 1995

Wasserstein, Bernard, *Britain and the Jews of Europe 1939-1945,* Leicester University Press, London 1999

Wilcock, Evelyn, *Pacifism and the Jews,* Hawthorn Press, Stroud 1994

Zahn, Gordon, *In Solitary Witness: the Life and Death of Franz Jägerstätter,* Templegate Publications; Springfield 1986 Rev. Ed.

Index